Amazing
Tales
of God's
Work *in*
an Ancient
Land

SILK ROAD
STORIES

Compiled *and* Edited *by*
Mark *&* Lynda Hausfeld
with Ken Horn

Silk Road Stories
Amazing Tales of God's Work in an Ancient Land
Compiled and Edited by Mark and Lynda Hausfeld
with Ken Horn

Second Printing

Printed in the United States of America
ISBN: 1-880689-13-8
Copyright 2007, Onward Books, Inc.

Cover design by Matt Key
Cover photography by Ken Horn

Scripture quotations are taken from the *New International Version*, Copyright 1973, 1978, 1984, International Bible Society.

The majority of the names in this book have been changed in order to protect individuals in sensitive countries and situations. Some aspects of characters and events have also been altered for the same reasons.

DEDICATION

To Jim and Dorothy Bryant, for pioneering the work in Central Eurasia, and for the selfless precedent you set for ministry in these lands.

To Jerry and Karen Parsley, for the godly leadership, support and freedom you give visionaries in these frontier harvest places.

Mark and Lynda Hausfeld

CONTENTS

* *Author names marked with an asterisk are pen names used for security reasons.*

FOREWORD

God is doing some amazing things in our world today. These are all the more noteworthy because of the great challenges that exist. In some cases the challenges have never been greater. There are countries that have had a near total vacuum of information about the greatest message the world has ever heard, the gospel of Jesus Christ. I believe that one of God's great purposes is to reach across our globe to those nations and peoples who have had limited access to this life-transforming message. It is, of course, our purpose to partner with Christ in taking this message to restricted countries—particularly where nations are ruled by Islam.

Two years in a row I had the privilege of visiting nations along the old Silk Road route, the area that we call Central Eurasia. In the process of those trips, I saw first-hand not only the tremendous challenges but also the high caliber of those servants of the Master who have taken up those challenges. I have the greatest admiration for our missionaries who put their lives in harm's way almost every day to be faithful to God's calling upon their lives. They are bringing the light of the gospel to some of the darkest places on earth.

I have also been privileged to meet great national leaders whom God has raised up to lead His work alongside our missionaries. In each of these countries there is a wonderful dynamic of anointed missionaries working closely with nationals passionate about Jesus.

I believe God is getting ready to do something big. There is expectancy in the air about God's purpose for this hour. I believe with all of my heart this is the moment for these lands. After many years of political and religious domination, they now have a window of opportunity to be exposed to the full message of Jesus Christ.

The book you are about to read contains true stories of what is happening in the countries on the Silk Road. You will meet inspiring people with stirring testimonies. I know they will be an inspiration to you. I pray they will also remind you that we need to pray more than we ever have before for the redemption of humankind in these lands. I believe it is possible, and I believe now is the time.

L. John Bueno
Executive Director
Assemblies of God World Missions

ACKNOWLEDGEMENTS

Special thanks to Matt Key, Shirley Speer, Peggy Horn, and Niki Pontou.

An ancient fort in Tajikistan

INTRODUCTION

The terms Church and Silk Road are seldom thought of together. Somehow they don't seem to fit. But they do . . . in surprising ways.

The Silk Road has been called "the bridge between Eastern and Western cultures." To residents of Western countries that bridge is needed. The Orient remains largely a mystery to us. The story of the Church that we know so well is really only the story of the Church in the West. There is another vast expanse of the globe with a powerful history and promising future for the Church.

Actually, the name Silk Road is somewhat of a misnomer. It is not one road, but many. Centuries ago, multiple routes crisscrossed Central Eurasia, linking a variety of eastern and western termini. One branch crossed the Pamir Mountains to Samarkand, Uzbekistan; another crossed the Tien Shan range, went through Tashkent, Uzbekistan, and eventually reached the shores of the Caspian Sea. The Silk Road linked the Yellow River

Valley of China with Byzantium (later Constantinople, today Istanbul, Turkey), a city that sits astride Asia and Europe.

Even the "Silk" part of the name is somewhat misleading. Besides the major barter of silk along the route, other goods were traded, including ivory, gold and even animals.

The Church of the East has a rich history, yet it remains relatively obscure. The Silk Road countries were once home to a thriving Christian movement, but warfare and persecution caused the worship of God to be replaced by an array of false deities, pushing the church to near extinction.

Let's take a glimpse at the history of the Eastern Church. Its history of victories, struggles and utter devastation sheds light on the Church's present condition—a golden epoch of harvest with immense potential, buffeted by great challenges.

The Church in the East looks from Jerusalem toward the sunrise. The history of this Church is filled with success and sorrow. Beginning at the Day of Pentecost (Acts 2:1-12), peoples of the East such as Parthians, Elamites and Medes from present-day Iran gathered in Jerusalem. Others present who heard the praises of God in their own tongues on that feast day were from Cappadocia, Pontus, Phrygia, and Pamphylia in today's Turkey. Scripture also says that people from "Asia" were present there and declared with the others that "we hear . . . the wonders of God in our own tongues" (Acts 2:11, NIV). Only God knows if those who were there returned to their peoples with stories of what they had heard and experienced in Jerusalem at that unique Feast of Weeks. However, history does tell us that if that they did not, others followed them and intentionally followed Jesus' command to "be my witnesses to the ends of the earth" (Acts 1:8b).

The earliest disciples of Jesus Christ from the first to the seventh centuries faithfully took the gospel to the Central Eurasian nations of Turkey, Azerbaijan, Iran, Uzbekistan, Turkmenistan, Kazakhstan, Tajikistan, Kyrgyzstan, Pakistan and Afghanistan. During the first 700 years the Church of the East, as it was called then, spread from Mt. Zion to beyond China. From the age of the apostles to the time of Muhammad cities along the routes that would become known as the Silk Roads became bastions of the Church that sent missionaries to people who had yet to hear the gospel. The ancient footprints of those missionaries left the imprint of the Prince of Peace among some of the most intolerant and violent peoples of that day.

Our brothers and sisters of over a millennium and a

half ago were compelled by the love of Christ to plant the Church. You will find evidence of their faithfulness if you visit the location of the old bazaar in Baku, Azerbaijan. There are stone crosses that indicate that at one time the body of Christ was present and active there. Farther east on the Silk Road, before meeting up with the majestic Tien Shan Mountains, one finds seventh-century cemeteries in the city of Tokmok, Kyrgyzstan. Recently, in the same area, archaeologists discovered the foundations of a church from the 11th century. One church historian writes:

"By the end of the second century, missionary expansion had carried the Church as far as Bactria in what is now northern Afghanistan, and mass conversions of Huns and Turks in central Asia were reported from the fifth century onward. By the end of the seventh century, Persian (Iranian) missionaries had reached the end of the world, the capital of the T'ang-dynasty China."[1]

If the story of the Church of the East ended at that point, it would be a success story and point to a prosperous future. Sadly, the eighth century would see that same Church suffer devastating loss. Moffett explains that "by then a cloud from the desert, Islam, was about to bring this first period of Asian church history crashing to a close."[2]

The rise of Islam is not the only cause for the near demise of the Eastern Church. Its turbulent history can also be attributed to "geographic isolation, chronic numerical weakness, persecution, the encounter with formidable Asian religions, ethnic introversion, dependence on the state and the church's own internal divisions."[3] Many of these factors are still present 13 centuries later.

Today the disadvantages of the past are still potential hazards, but it is a new day for the Church in the East. No longer is Central Eurasia isolated geographically. The Internet and satellite communications have seen to that. In the place of chronic weakness in numbers, the Church in Asia is growing faster than in the West, though Christians still only make up 3.5 percent of the population of Asia.[4] Persecution is still a very real problem in Central Eurasia, but where today's Church faces hostility, the body of Christ grows the most. Asian religions are still the majority faiths along the Silk Roads, but now more than ever peoples are leaving their ancestral faiths, believing on Christ alone for eternal life, and becoming part of the community of faith. Ethnic separation between believers is not the issue in the Church that it was in the past. State support for the Pentecostal Church is nonexistent, so money does not politicize Church leadership. Finally, the Church, though not perfect, is seeking the unity of spirit and the bonds of peace. Jesus said, "I will build my church, and the gates of hell shall not prevail against it" (Matthew 16:18, KJV).

This book is a compilation of exciting stories of real people who have been dramatically touched by God. These testimonies are just a handful of the many that could be told. God is indeed at work along Central Eurasia's old Silk Roads, moving by His Spirit through His Church. Our purpose in this book is threefold: (1) to testify to these great works of God in the awakening Eastern Church; (2) to influence believers to pray for this part of the world; and (3) to convey the need for laborers in these great nations.

Today, first generation believers are building a first generation church in Central Eurasia. As you read, open your heart to the compelling people you will meet. And allow the Holy Spirit to be your Guide . . . along the Silk Road.

Mark Hausfeld

Endnotes

1. Samuel Hugh Moffett, *A History of Christianity in Asia, Volume 1: Beginnings to 1500* (Maryknoll, New York: Orbis Books, 1998), xv

2. Moffett, xv

3. Moffett, 503

4. Patrick Johnstone and Jason Mandryk, *Operation World: 21st Century Edition* (Waynesboro, GA: Paternoster Publishing, 2001), 42

Silk Road Countries

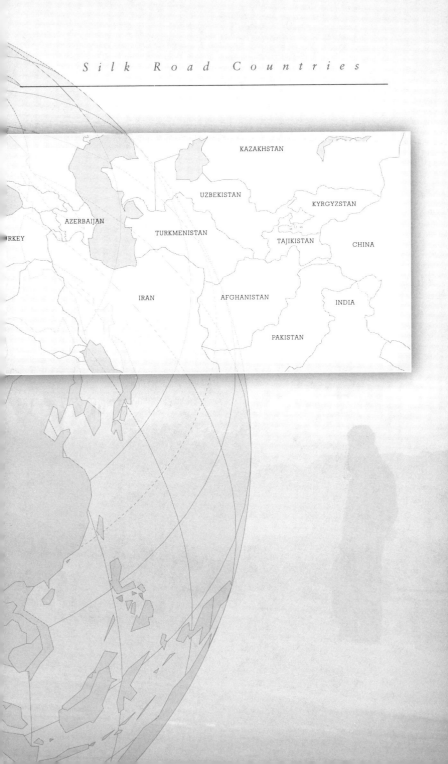

KAZAKHSTAN

UZBEKISTAN

KYRGYZSTAN

TAJIKISTAN

CHINA

AFGHANISTAN

PAKISTAN

INDIA

Beshenbek

Chapter One

BESHENBEK'S VISION

By David Broberg

One thousand years ago, Christians lived along the Silk Road. I have walked the ruins of ninth- and 10th-century Nestorian churches in Kyrgyzstan where I live. But the gospel message never reached the nomadic yurts and villages in the foothills of the Himalayan Mountains of Central Eurasia.

After the Iron Curtain fell and Central Eurasia opened to the gospel message, Silk Road Bible College (now Silk Road Theological Institute) was established in 1996 to train pastors and leaders for the churches of Central Eurasia. Russian is a common language throughout the former Soviet Union and all education was taught in this language. Kyrgyz, spoken by the nomadic Kyrgyz people, became a written language only about 100 years ago and has never been used in education. It is thought here that educated people study in Russian.

But soon non-Russian-speaking village people came to the cities—Tokmok, Kara Balta, Kara Kol, and Bishkek—and met Christians and committed their lives to God. A 28-year-old single Kyrgyz man came to Bishkek. After attending church and receiving his first Bible, he decided to accept Christ. At that time, we decided to offer a one-year program at Silk Road Bible College in Kyrgyz for these non-Russian speakers. So, Beshenbek came to us as a young Christian who had heard from God and was determined to reach his people with the hope of salvation through Jesus Christ.

Beshenbek was a poor student. But he studied hard and seemed to be a serious Christian. So we helped him with tutors and extra credit work and he became a straight "C" student. I smile now as I remember thinking that our mission at Silk Road is to prepare workers for the harvest field and not Harvard graduates. So, if Beshenbek can preach the gospel to his people, who have no hope, then our mission is complete. As the time came for the year to finish, Beshenbek brought me the following letter:

"Greetings to you and your family. I want you to know me, so I am writing my biography. I was born in the south in a village. I wasn't very good at school, because I didn't even speak Kyrgyz well and so only attended through the eighth grade. I then became a shepherd in the mountains and had no hope for my life. Then I went to Bishkek and met Christians. They gave me a Bible and I began to read it. They told me how to become a believer and I repented and God filled my heart. Now there was hope.

"God gave me a vision of a room full of people and I was sitting in the back. A man was speaking, who I didn't know. Out the window, I could see poplar trees blowing in the wind. I didn't know the room, the people or the man. God also began to speak to me about beginning a church in my village in the mountains. I spoke to my pastor and he agreed, but said that I needed to attend Silk Road Bible College first, so I came to the college. When I attended the chapel services, I realized that you were the man in my vision and the room was the chapel at Silk Road. God confirmed I was following Him.

"Now I am going to graduate and want to thank you and many others who have helped, encouraged and taught me. I will go to my village, because they also live without hope. The people in the nearest villages are also waiting for salvation. I promise you that I will be faithful even when it's slow."

At graduation, Beshenbek's name was called first and I remember his walking the aisle to receive his certificate. He was the first graduate of a Bible College in the Kyrgyz language in history.

The graduates went back to their homes and we didn't hear from Beshenbek for two years. His pastor told me that he was back in his village establishing a church.

Then, after two years, he appeared at my office door. I was so happy to see him and to hear what was happening in his ministry. He sat down and after lengthy greetings concerning our families, I asked him about his ministry.

He smiled and said, "My uncle died." Why was he smiling? Then he said, "And I inherited his house and we are making it into a church."

"How many believers do you have?"

"Four families," Beshenbek said.

Praise God! Four families in a village of 2,000 people in the mountains of southern Kyrgyzstan. The gospel had never been preached there before.

Beshenbek had more news. He and some friends were going to the other villages also, because they have never heard the gospel and have no hope.

God still calls and uses shepherd boys.

A Central Eurasian shepherd

People of Kyrgyzstan

Nargiza

Chapter Two

NARGIZA'S NIGHTMARE
As told to David Broberg

My name is Nargiza. I'm 20 years old.

I was born into an educated Muslim family, the fourth of five children. We loved and respected our parents. They brought us up in the ways of Islam. My father was highly educated—he had earned four degrees. An animal geneticist, he was also a chief administrator and an *akim* (like a local mayor). We respected him as though he was god. He was kind, humble and good to people. I wanted to enter the Islamic institute very much, but entered another one as a designer.

Our father was the only hope and light in our family. Suddenly, in 2001, when he was 50, we lost him. Former associates from Iraq and Afghanistan killed him after he refused to become involved in their intrigues. Our family lived with a sense of impending danger.

I lost any hope and sense of life. I cried out to God. "It wasn't fair. Why did You take my father? He never failed me." Our family was in great depression. Every day we sobbed and wept. I left my family and my studies.

I met a group of young people who used drugs, drank and smoked. They were from rich families and they rented an apartment for me. At night I would call my father's spirit and talk with him. I was going crazy. If I had done this a few days more I would have been admitted to a mental hospital.

God sent His mercy to me in the form of a person who showed me the truth about salvation in Jesus. I told God, "Here are my hands and feet and mouth; take everything and forgive me. I want to receive healing." From that moment He became my Father, Brother and Friend. God saved me just in time. I returned home.

It was my great desire to study in a religious seminary. I fasted and prayed every day, and God sent me to Silk Road Bible College in Bishkek. I grew in the Lord there and my future looked bright. Jesus was the only important one for me. After successfully completing the first course I returned home, strong spiritually and cheerful and in my mind. I thought I could change the world. I was greatly anticipating the second year.

But something terrible happened. It was the summer of 2003. I was kidnapped and forced to marry a man I didn't know who was eight years older than I. I struggled, but I didn't fight. I wanted to behave as a Christian.

I had been taken to a remote village, where people weren't educated. My husband had paid 8,000 soms ($175) for me. I lived in a dirty shed. My husband drank a lot and two days after the wedding he beat me. I seemed so far from God. I couldn't even pray.

They knew that I was a believer. The house became my prison. I worked from morning till night as a slave.

My husband often became drunk and beat me. He frequently threatened to kill me if I didn't leave God. One night he took me to a nearby lake. "Right now, you leave God, otherwise I will drown you." Somehow God protected me. My husband tried a number of other times.

Then one day the family gave me a choice: "Choose God or us."

"I choose God," I said.

So they gave me a noose and ordered me to hang myself. So great was their power and my misery that I went off alone and obeyed. I had hung for some 25 seconds when the rope broke. I fell to the ground and lay there one and a half hours.

A woman found me and helped me up. Blood was flowing from my nose and I couldn't speak. The noose had choked my voice away. This kind woman paid a taxi to take me to Bishkek.

In Bishkek a pastor I knew gave me a place to live. He prayed for me and encouraged me. He wept with me and helped me restore my life. God gave my voice back. We prayed for God to give me a chance to study at college again. God answered and on September 1, I returned to Silk Road Bible College. It was a miracle.

I don't know why these things happened to me. But I believe when it is the right time, I'll receive answers to my questions. The most important thing is that I'm with Jesus and I'm closer to God. He has turned my nightmare into joy.

I was very happy to be reunited with my brothers and sisters at the college again. Here I changed, grew up and was restored. Every minute at the college was precious to me. My goal in life is to serve Muslim families and humiliated women in Asia.

Editor's note: After graduation in 2004, Nargiza moved to Jahalad Abad in southern Kyrgyzstan, and is working in the Kudai Jamaatee, an Assemblies of God church in that city.

A Kyrgyz woman

A Kyrgyz farmer

*Women worship in
an outdoor church
in Central Eurasia*

Ancient minaret in Kyrgzstan

3

*Afghan men at a school for
children of refugees*

Chapter Three

FORMER MUJAHADEEN FINDS THE LORD

*By Timothy Virnon**

Working with Afghans for nearly 10 years has brought us into contact with all sorts of very interesting people. We have worked or come in contact with government officials—including turbaned Taliban leaders when the Taliban held sway in Afghanistan, white-bearded village elders and scowling, suspicious mullahs. (Most of the time, mullahs were very uncomfortable around us "foreigners.") There were simple farmers, university professors, Islamic "holy men," beggar ladies completely engulfed in sky-blue burqas[1] holding babies who looked at us with big brown eyes. There were the little shoe-shine boys who hung around looking for handouts and friendship (practicing their broken English and spying for the Taliban intelligence), wily shopkeepers who constantly "adjusted" their prices to get the best deal possible. It was an endless adventure unlike anything I had ever experienced before.

Among this array of interesting people was my good friend Javed, the very first Afghan that I met upon arriving in Afghanistan.

When we arrived in Afghanistan, we stayed initially at the house of a co-worker who was away on holiday. Javed was the *chowkidar*, or guard, who watched over the house. In Afghan culture it is quite normal to employ a *chowkidar*, and the *chowkidar* often becomes a bit of a do-it-all person for the family. Javed was an expert at shopping, washing dishes, ironing clothes, driving a car, keeping the garden, and most importantly, providing the fierce Afghan protection and watchfulness that was sometimes needed to keep away thieves and other bad people. He also was a pretty good language helper as we learned the local tongue.

Javed had been a Mujahed[2] who had fought during the 1980s with the Afghan resistance against the forces of the Soviet Union. But, by the time we met him, Javed had settled down a bit. He now had a family, including four daughters. In Afghan culture, sons are most desirable, and daughters are not always very welcome. Sometimes, when a daughter is born there is little celebration. The wife may even apologize to her husband for giving birth to a girl instead of a boy. When a son is born, however, there is usually a party! Male friends and relatives may shoot off guns into the air. There may be music and dancing and delicious *sheeranay* or sweets for everyone. Javed did not seem to be too upset that he had only daughters, which made him a little unusual for an Afghan.

Javed lived in a very simple mud house in a village not too far from where we were living. He rode his bicycle into town every morning and back to his village on most evenings. Sometimes he stayed at the house overnight— even for several nights if there were security problems in our area (which happened from time to time during the Civil War and Taliban years).

Javed rode back and forth nearly five miles each way on dirt roads. If it rained the roads were a mess of mud and ruts and it was difficult for him to make the trip. But he was always cheerful and never complained about his circumstances.

On our first night in Afghanistan our family was getting used to all the exciting sights, sounds and smells of our new home. And there were plenty of new things to experience!

For one, it took us a long time to get used to sharing the road, not only with other vehicles, but with all sorts of interesting traffic. There were horse-drawn carts (tongas), and small, motorized three-wheeled taxis called rickshaws that putted along beside you throwing off lots of smelly smoke and sounding like a lawn mower on wheels. There were occasional herds of sheep, each with its barefoot, dirty shepherd boy or girl armed with little sticks. Big diesel trucks were often loaded with smuggled goods. They bore paintings of elaborate and beautiful landscapes that looked like Switzerland (about as far from dusty, brown, hot Afghanistan as you can get). Or they carried the names of German beer breweries—quite a shock to see in a Muslim country where drinking alcohol is a big sin. (These big, used trucks came from Germany and no one bothered to paint over the beautiful German letters.) There were little donkeys often hauling loads of bricks or sand that seemed much too large for their sturdy little backs. Long, slim gasoline tankers carried creative warning signs reading "Dinger! Patrolum! Hugly Inframble!" or variations that made you laugh and laugh. (The signs are supposed to read "Dangerous Petroleum—Highly Inflammable.")

And that first sunset we had our first experience of "dueling mullahs" as (to our regret) we found that our house was equidistant from three different mosques! The mullahs all had loudspeakers, cranked up very loud (after all, this was the call to prayer). They were obviously competing with each other to pack their respective mosques during the prayer times. The loudest one we called "the screamer." It is impossible to describe the exquisite sensations we had as this mullah literally screamed out his "yell" to prayer. Later, there were times that I mused about trying to see if it would be appropriate to have someone come and give singing lessons to "the screamer." I am sure that all in the neighborhood would have been very happy.

We also all jumped when we heard several long bursts of noise that made a crisp, loud sound like "bbbrrrrrrrrrtttt"—and not very far away, either. We asked our host if that was the sound of Kalishnakov fire, which we had heard so much about. We were told that it was—and probably represented a demonstration of joy at the birth of a baby boy or a wedding or some other happy occasion. Later we heard stories that illustrated the immutable law of physics that "what goes up, must come down"—stories of people being pierced and even killed by this Afghan "friendly fire."

As our first evening in Afghanistan wound down, I stepped outside to enjoy a bit of the cooling night air. Out of the darkness, Javed came toward me shouting in broken English. (I did not yet know his mother tongue—Pashto.) "Mr. Vernon, Mr. Vernon, come, come," he said, taking me by the hand. (In the Middle East and in Central and Southern Asia men often walk together holding hands—a real culture shock for this suburban city-dweller from Chicago!) He pulled me toward the *hujra* or guest room, where visitors were usually entertained and endless cups of sweet green tea were consumed. As we headed toward the *hujra*, I noticed that Javed had a videocassette in his other hand. (I think the one holding my hand was getting quite sweaty by this time.)

We entered the *hujra* and Javed popped the cassette into the VCR and turned on the small TV. We sat on the thin, red *toshaks* (mattresses) that were spread on the floor around the room. (I still get the wonderful tingling feeling as my legs, unaccustomed to such sitting, fall asleep while squatting on these low, flat cushions.) Javed was talking to me now mostly in his Pashto, but I did hear the word "Isa" several times—which is the Arabic word for Jesus. To my great surprise, Javed and I began to watch the unfolding first scenes of the Jesus film—all in Pashto. Javed was so excited. "Mr. Virnon, thees ees Mariam (Mary) and Yusuf (Joseph)" and "He ees YahYa al Salam" as I saw a hairy John the Baptist (he looked a lot like Javed actually) standing in the Jordan River. The electricity cut out, as it does often, and we didn't get very far into the film, but I remember walking back into the kitchen in a bit of a daze.

All this on our first day in the country! It was almost too much to absorb.

In fact, I was a very confused man. How could it be possible for an Afghan like Javed to show me the *Jesus* film? That was something I would never have expected to happen—especially from someone whom I did not really know! I later found out that Javed was a devout Muslim, and that he had been a fighter with the Mujahadeen. But, like many Afghans who saw the *Jesus* film, Javed loved the story and he had begun to fall in love with Jesus. He loved to show the film to other Afghans too, even to his old Mujahadeen friends.

A few days after my first encounter with Javed, we moved into our own house a few doors away, but I saw him often as I regularly visited the house where he was the *chowkidar*.

One day, a couple of years later, Javed came to see me. He was upset. His newest baby (another daughter) was very sick. She had been running a high fever for a few days and had not been nursing. He said that when he left his house, she was hardly moving.

I felt strongly impressed to do something I had not ever done before. I told Javed that I was going to lay my hands on his hands and pray for his daughter to be healed in Jesus' name. Javed had been prayed for many times, and he knew that God often answered our prayers, so he quickly agreed. As I put my hands on his, I sensed a powerful presence of the Holy Spirit. I prayed with unusual fluency for me—a prayer for healing in Pashto—

and I knew Javed felt the presence of the Lord too. When I finished praying, I felt prompted to tell Javed to go home immediately, lay his own hands on his sick daughter, and pray the same prayer over her that I had just prayed. Javed quickly left.

The next morning, as I was working at my office, I heard a buzz of conversation outside in the garden that became louder as it moved toward where I was. I caught a few words like, "*Loya Mojeza Dey!*"—"It is a Great Miracle." And "*Da Xoday Barakat Dey!*"—"This is God's Blessing!" A beaming Javed walked into my room and I quickly understood what the commotion was all about. Javed had done what I told him to do, and his daughter had recovered almost immediately! By the end of the day, the fever was gone and his baby daughter was eating, playing and laughing. He was so excited and thankful to God for healing his daughter. Even the other Afghans working in the office were sharing in his joy.

A few weeks later another friend prayed for Javed when he himself was sick, and he was also healed by the Lord. He then gave his heart to Jesus—and shortly after this he came and told me all about it. What blessed fellowship we had!

A short time later, again after specific, believing prayer, Javed's wife became pregnant and later gave birth to their first son. What a privilege to see one of my friends encounter the living Jesus Christ in such a powerful way.

I could tell many other stories about Javed. But I will only say that today Javed is one of the key believers in our area. He has helped a number of his friends to come to know Jesus and he is growing and maturing as a leader. His testimony is one that could be multiplied hundreds of times as our tough, yet somehow tender-hearted friends encounter our wonderful Lord Jesus as He travels along the Silk Road.

Endnotes

1. Burqa—The traditional all-covering robe with a cloth screen over the eyes that all Afghan women were required to wear during the Taliban time.

2. Arabic word meaning "holy warrior."

A villager at his home that was bombed by the Taliban

Land mine victim

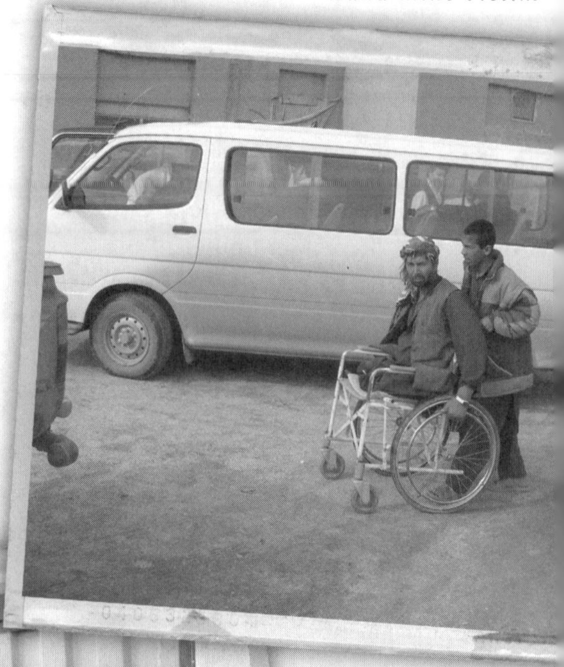

Afghan in Kabul

Young Afghan with calf

Akram

THE INVISIBLE WALL

*By Peyton Alan**

One month before we arrived in Central Eurasia, a young Uighur (pronounced "oo-wee-gur") man saw the film *Jesus*. Anvar was so moved that he accepted some of the free Christian literature that was distributed at the theater. Upon returning home, he was greeted by his oldest brother who was visiting. His brother reacted violently when he saw the Christian literature, beating his younger brother viciously. "Remember," he warned him, "our father is a mullah [a Muslim holy man]. Don't bring shame on our family."

Anvar retreated to his bedroom, sad and frustrated. "If You really sent Jesus to die for me," Anvar prayed, "then please send someone to tell me about Him." One month later we moved into his apartment building.

Anvar befriended us right away. We could barely speak Russian, and his English vocabulary was limited to "It's

OK." Somehow we communicated. He was a hairstylist so he offered to cut my hair. Later he invited our family to his home for a special pasta dish. His father, the mullah, was also a wonderful cook and a musician. We enjoyed many wonderful meals with Anvar and his father, Akram.

After three months, Anvar asked me if I were a Christian. Instead of merely saying "Yes" and perhaps missing a moment to define what Christianity really is, I gave him a long answer: "I believe in Jesus, the Messiah ["Messiah" is an easier term for Muslims than the Greek term "Christ"]. I believe that Jesus died and came back to life again."

Anvar then shocked me by nodding in agreement and asking if he could be a Christian, too. I tried to explain more of the gospel, but my command of Russian was too limited. So I went back to my apartment and retrieved a copy of the Four Spiritual Laws in Russian. We looked at the tract together, and within a few minutes, Anvar was praying the "sinner's prayer."

Akram, the mullah, was not angry, but instead thanked me for being a positive influence on Anvar. I sincerely enjoyed my times of fellowship with Anvar, Akram, and others who came into the home. The oldest son, however, was not pleased with me at all. It was rare for the two of us to visit at the same time.

Often during our visits, Akram would play exotic
musical instruments and sing. He had sung all over China.
On top of that, while a youth, he had been a freedom
fighter for the Uighur resistance against the Chinese (so,
to the Chinese government, he was a "terrorist"). Akram
called me his "American son," and he loved me like a son.

Akram and his family were poor. Yet, whenever I visited,
they would feed me. After we moved to another part of
the city, I continued to visit a few times every month. Each
time Akram would feed me something. On one occasion
I felt that I should plan my visit in between meal times,
so I arrived at 4:00 p.m. Akram had just prepared a plate
full of rice and mutton. He handed me another fork and
we ate out of the same plate. He made sure that I had the
choicest pieces of meat and fat.

Usually we spent hours talking and drinking tea
(which was therapeutic after eating the choice pieces
of fat). And on many of these occasions, I would try to
share something about Isa (the Muslim name for Jesus).
But whenever I mentioned the name, Akram would
immediately say, gently, "Peyton, Isa was only a prophet,
just like Muhammad and Elijah." Then he would open his
Koran and begin to read to us from it. It was as though an
invisible wall would suddenly be erected between us, and I
could never cross over with the story of Jesus.

Three years after our first encounter, Akram became sick. After a time in the hospital and at his daughter's home in another part of the city, he came back to his apartment for his last month. I visited him with greater frequency, and it was obvious that his strength was fading. I tried to speak about Jesus, but the same invisible wall would be erected. I was getting nowhere.

One evening, Anvar called and informed me that his father had been in a coma for about two days. The doctor had declared that Akram would not live through the night. The whole apartment was full of family; they were all Muslims. Anvar said he felt alone and wanted me to come and be with him. I took a taxi to his home, where I found a room full of beautiful, but sad, Uighurs, dressed in black. The man who had prayed over their children and at the funerals of their parents and grandparents . . . the one who had taught them from the Koran was about to die. There is no assurance of salvation in Islam, and the looks on their faces showed this. I shook hands with all the men, and then Anvar took me to see his father. Akram was lying completely still; he was barely breathing. They shook him gently and said, "Peyton is here." But there was no response. I stared at my Uighur father with tears in my eyes. This man loved me like a son. He had sought God all his life, but only knew the God of Islam. He was now about to enter eternity without Jesus—and that would mean hell.

I bowed my head and placed my hand on Akram's shoulder. I prayed, even though I wasn't sure what to pray. Then suddenly I had a thought. While it might be too late for Akram, it was not too late for the Muslims in the other room. I would tell Akram about Jesus now (he couldn't object), and the people in the next room would hear the gospel for the first time. I opened my eyes and saw the oldest son had come into the room with me. Therefore I asked his permission before I spoke to Akram.

I purposefully took about five minutes to ask the question. "May I tell your father why I have confidence that when I die I will be in heaven because of the death and resurrection of Isa?" I told the whole gospel in the question. The older son looked at me and said, "No."

I was disappointed, but I knew I had at least shared the gospel with the whole house. I remained by Akram's side and prayed.

Suddenly, without warning, Akram spoke. With a strained voice he said to me, "You may!" This time there was no invisible wall, and I was actually being invited by a mullah to tell him the gospel. The older son stormed off to another room, but I bent towards Akram. I told him again about Isa's love, sacrifice and resurrection. I encouraged him to repent of his sins and believe on Isa.

That was the last thing that Akram heard, and within an hour he was gone. I believe that those last moments were the most critical for Akram's salvation. I believe that he is now singing in the heavenly choir.

Women workers

Tea time

61

*Musicians with
drums and sitar*

*Ceremonial
washing prior
to entering
mosque*

TRANSFORMATION:

An abode of sorrow and death becomes a place of light and life

By Mike and Cindy

"Who am I?" I scream in the cold darkness, left on the floor to lie alone, no warm arms around me, left to live and die in my own waste. In my whole life I receive no tender touches, no one smiles at me, and no one is ever glad to see me. I have this hunger for something more than food, something that has remained unknown to me but I need so badly. I hurt for it, I ache for it. What is love? Please tell me what it looks like because I've never seen or known it. Can you imagine how I feel?

Mike's Perspective

In 1994 my wife, Cindy, found a garbage can that was called an "orphanage." A garbage can where mentally and physically challenged children were thrown away. They

died every week, unknown, forgotten. Those who survived
writhed on the floor in pain, anger and fear, their lives
filled with their own pain and the pain of the children who
screamed on the floor beside them. The only adult in their
lives was a woman who sat in a chair with a stick and
beat them if they dared to inconvenience her. The children
did not know their names . . . they thought their names
were the curse words the orphanage workers called them.
When Cindy first tried to hug them they became afraid
because the only human touch they knew was a stick that
beat them.

Before this, we had worked in India. I remember
the long lines of lepers waiting for Cindy to clean and
bandage their wounds. I thought she had seen everything.
Then came the orphanage. After working all day at the
orphanage, she would keep me awake at night, crying
about what she had seen.

So I went to the orphanage. And I wept uncontrollably
as I watched my wife enter filthy rooms reeking with
human waste to love and care for children while I could
only stand at the door and gag from the smell.

It was here we realized how very necessary is the prayer
support of our friends and churches. We asked them to
pray . . . and God started working.

For a year and a half Cindy worked at the orphanage alone. Then God began to give her national Christian sisters to help her. We now have 76 national Christian women caregivers showing the love of Jesus to the children.

Children like Gulnoza. Gulnoza was bedridden, a 12-year-old girl who had never moved or spoken. One of our caregivers began to massage her legs and pray for her. Gulnoza did not respond. The sister began to play worship music as she massaged and prayed for her. Some months went by and Gulnoza began making sounds. She was humming the tunes of the worship songs. Later, she began forming the words of the songs with her lips. And then, she sat up and started singing them!

A government worker heard her and told her she was an idiot and didn't know what she was singing. Gulnoza answered, "I know God loves me and will take me to a better place."

Gulnara was one of the few orphans who survived. She was an angry young teenager when I first saw her, covered with scars and unable to speak. She thought her name was a curse word. One of our caregivers, a speech therapist, spent a lot of time with Gulnara teaching her to speak. Gulnara asked Jesus to forgive her and live in her heart. When the government workers would call her a curse word she would answer, "That's not my name. My name is Gulnara." Gulnara means flower.

Christina is now a young lady. When she was younger she was beaten so badly at the orphanage that she went blind. She talks about how angry she was at the people who took her sight away. When she gave her life to Jesus she was able to forgive them and live in the joy of God's love.

Now when I go to the orphanage I still weep. Only now I weep for joy, for the beauty of God that I see in the children's lives. They did not know what love was but Jesus himself showed them—and now these special children show us His love. The caregivers and the children—together they are a picture of Jesus. A pastor who recently visited the orphanage said, "Everywhere I look I see Jesus!"

Cindy's Perspective

As the Light shines on this multifaceted precision cut crystal we stand in awe of the beautiful work of His hands.

What a wonderful work He has done in many of these precious lives. Some of the children have asked Jesus to come into their lives and to fill them with His Spirit. God has cancelled their fears and brought hope, healing them physically, mentally, and emotionally. The stories of Gulnoza, Gulnara, and Christina are just a few of many such testimonies, each one representing a life transformed by Christ and precious to Him.

But the testimonies of transformation are not limited to the orphans. God has also empowered the national Christian caregivers to be the women of God He intended them to be. He has healed many of their scars as well—scars left on them by abusive husbands and fathers. He has set them free, and opened their minds and hearts to minister to children that they did not even know existed before in their society, mentally and physically disabled children, who seemed to be "accidents" or "mistakes," outside of God's purposes and love. He has strengthened them as they have learned to be a team, a powerful prayer force together waiting, believing, and experiencing the miracles of God in their lives, in the lives of the children, and even in the lives of the government caregivers.

Some of these government orphanage staff have come to know the Lord as their Savior and are attending church. They freely share their faith with others. Though not all of these have come to the Lord, we are thankful that most of these have experienced a change of heart and attitude toward the children—loving them and seeing them as human beings with worth. With this change of attitude beatings have stopped; good care, personal touching and playing have become a part of everyday life.

There is even a remarkable testimony of God's goodness among our work crew. Originally, there were just a few brothers in the Lord who did maintenance and minor repairs. But God wanted the orphanage to be a work place of ministry. So He began to lay it on the hearts of our brothers to hire alcoholics and drug addicts, men who needed new life in Christ and discipleship. Daily they worked alongside them, and ministered to them as they worked. Now these young men are free from their bondages and have learned skills so they can make a living. From this beginning two cell churches have been birthed and two of the young men are now training to be pastors.

And so we continue to wait, pray and work. And as we do so we are grateful for the friends and churches who work here with us, and those who make this work possible. Everywhere we look at the orphanage we see Jesus and we see our friends' names, faces, and the fingerprints of their love.

Happy children of the transformed orphanage

Bishop Sergie

UZBEKISTAN AND BEYOND WITH BISHOP SERGIE

As told to Ken Horn

Tashkent, Uzbekistan's capital, is in the foothills of the Tien Shan Mountains. The largest and one of the oldest cities of Central Eurasia, Tashkent lies in a great oasis along the Trans-Caspian Railroad, bordered by the Chirchiq River. It was one of the republics of the former Soviet Union, receiving an uneasy independence when the Iron Curtain fell.

Tashkent is significant for more than geography or history. It is the headquarters of Bishop Sergie, Ukrainian church planter extraordinaire. Much of what God is doing along the Silk Road today can be traced back to Tashkent.

Full Gospel Center

Every morning believers congregate for the daily prayer meeting at Full Gospel Center, the thriving church of

4,000 that Sergie planted and that Alex, a disciple of Sergie, now pastors.

A beautiful sense of God's presence is evident at the meetings. Early morning sunlight pours through high windows, bathing the intercessors in light. People pray in varying postures. Some kneel, others sit, and some walk the aisles. All are fervent. At the meeting's close, a leader steps to the front and the group recites the Apostles' Creed.

This is the power plant of the Uzbekistan church. Every Monday the prayer meeting lasts all day. Once a demon-possessed man wandered in. When he left, he had been delivered from demons and was born again.

Building a church of this size—of any size—is not without its challenges in this part of the former Soviet Union. Churches face difficulties receiving official recognition. Even when registered they endure close scrutiny.

This particular day there is a second meeting—a special one for pastors. Many have come from great distances and met numerous obstacles just to be here. One pastor's 500-kilometer trip included numerous checkpoints "just as if we were coming from another country," he says.

This meeting is the beginning of a remarkable whirlwind tour of Uzbekistan, led by Sergie, for several American church leaders. Three languages—Russian, Uzbek and Tatar—are spoken and sung at the meeting. Once an unreached people group, Tatars now number enough believers that their language is frequently heard in Uzbek church services.

A pastor's report of victory in his remote region is received enthusiastically. "Our church is 10 years old," he says. "No believers lived in our town before that. Now God is doing miracles."

One diminutive pastor is considered an "apostle Paul of Uzbekistan." Slight of stature like the apostle, he is also similar in his courage, pioneering in difficult areas that are averse to the gospel. He travels regularly to several churches he has planted and has an expansive vision to continue making inroads into the devil's territory.

Pastors stand and share victories and challenges. There are many of both. It is a special time for all, probably much like the persecuted church leaders of the first century coming together in the Roman Empire to share how the church was growing.

Healing testimonies are common. As with the Early Church, these men are familiar with signs and wonders, and they are thoroughly Pentecostal. A pastor from another distant city tells of an outpouring among children. "We have seen children as young as 12 filled with the Holy Spirit," he beams.

Pastor Sergie and this congregation have been instrumental in most of these success stories, planting some 120 churches in the area. Fifty-three languages are represented in Sergie's church alone. Sergie is adamant that no man or church is responsible for this growth. "The Holy Spirit is," he says.

But those who know this area best recognize the crucial role the Holy Spirit has tapped Bishop Sergie to play in the work. No one knows better than Mike:

"It is my privilege to know Pastor Sergie. He was born and raised in the Soviet system, a precious man God is using to turn the grayness and gloom of his country into blazing light. Pastor Sergie and his wife Tanya can tell you of many Christian family members who died in the labor camps. Yet Sergie and Tanya have not let circumstances shape them. In the power of the Holy Spirit they have turned their Central Asian country upside down. God has used him to plant churches and release hundreds of men and women into ministry. He is loved by the Uzbeks, Russians, Kazakhs, Karakalpaks and others who have come to Jesus through him.

"Pastor Sergie is a man with a burning passion for the Lord. Though in his early 50s, he has worked so relentlessly his physical health has been affected. We have worked together for ten years—the most privileged years of my life. Though intense, he has an incredible sense of humor and contagious laughter. He loves children and holds my wife's work with them in high regard. Once we were driving to the opening of a new church. On the way he noticed mulberry bushes ripe with berries. After the church opening and lunch he turned to the new pastor. 'Please bring me a bowl,' he asked. He drove straight to the mulberry bushes and, standing in ankle deep water, filled the bowl with berries. 'Mike, these are a present for Cindy,' he told me, 'since she could not come with us.' "

Quest for Souls

Sergie came from his native Ukraine and started his first church in Uzbekistan in 1986 with eight people. He ministered throughout the country and God called others to work alongside him. In 1990 there was a surge of growth—what Sergie calls "a spontaneous fountain from God. People were coming on their own," he says. "It was the work of the Holy Spirit. We would only say a few words and they were ready to receive Jesus."

Once, while traveling to evangelize in a distant city he had a flat tire and went to get it fixed. He witnessed to the mechanics in the shop. All of them gave their lives to Jesus. Things like this still happen frequently . . . a combination of the Holy Spirit's power and Sergie's indefatigable quest for souls.

Another effort did not seem so successful. Sergie evangelized in a small village for three days. But there were few results. He put the village out of his mind. Six years later, residents of the village contacted him. When he returned, he found that a vigorous church had sprung up.

"I forgot about them for six years," Sergie says, "but the Holy Spirit didn't forget about them."

Some of the churches planted by Pastor Sergie are in surrounding countries, such as Tajikistan, Kyrgyzstan and Kazakhstan. Thirty-two have successfully navigated the difficult waters of government registration; others choose to meet secretly because of the unceasing hassles recognized congregations can expect.

The explosion of souls coming to the Lord in the 1990s produced a problem. Every region of Uzbekistan now had a group of believers—mostly Uzbek, Kazakh and Karakalpak. But these large groups needed spiritual leaders. The growth had been so rapid, new believers were pressed into service. And there was nowhere in the country to train them.

"We had to send them to other countries for training," Sergie says. "Sometimes the schools would ask me, 'How many years have they been a Christian?' And I would answer, 'Three months.' They told me it was too early to send them but I told them I didn't have anyone else.

"God invited the people from the street to be saved," Sergie continues. "The church grew very strong, with many people. Today, in Tashkent alone, from our original church five large registered churches have been born. In Tashkent there are many other groups, house churches and Christians. Many more churches are not registered."

And today there is a seminary, though as yet unregistered.

Sergie expresses a debt of gratitude to workers from other countries, like Jim and Dorothy Bryant, the area's pioneer directors. "I thank the Lord for these wonderful and beautiful people," Sergie says. "They helped with any problem with all their hearts. At that time we had many hard difficulties; we couldn't get literature or build churches. But thanks to the Lord this brother participated in God's work. Because of this we became members of the Assemblies of God."

As the church grew, ministries were added. Christians began helping at hospitals, sanatoriums, and orphanages.

A ministry for newly released prisoners was begun. Many have been rehabilitated and become Christians and today are law-abiding citizens.

And Teen Challenge was begun. "God sent a wonderful brother, Travis," Sergie says. "He trained brother Victor who is an Uzbek citizen. They started a wonderful drug and alcohol rehabilitation center. Every Sunday morning at 7 a.m. a worship team of more than 15 ex-alcoholics and drug addicts are singing in worship to the Lord, with hands raised, praising God."

Sergie brings the group to the new center in Yangi, a village outside Tashkent. A crew of construction workers is hard at work as the group arrives.

Travis is a strapping Floridian with a ready smile, and his wife, Raushan, is a Kazakh. Among the hired workers are several who have given their lives to Christ since they came to work here.

The resident students all have duties, too. Slovah, in the program for six months, is grinding food for the animals.

The center currently owns two properties and has its eye on three others. "Our goal in this village," Travis says, "is to have a boys' program, a detox center, in addition to the men's Teen Challenge rehabilitation program."

Testimonies already abound. One of the worker's wives started attending night home group meetings. He found out about it and threatened to throw her out of the house. She stopped going, but a few months later she discovered that her husband, who was an alcoholic, had started attending the meetings himself. Within a month he gave his life to the Lord, and now his entire family is saved and serving Christ.

With alcoholism and drug abuse rampant, Teen Challenge centers have been welcomed in Central Eurasia.

The church has also organized medical outreaches with the many Christian doctors and nurses who are members. They treat sick people freely, dispensing free medicine. This opens the door for evangelism.

"We are reaching the farthest regions," says Sergie. "We are going where no one has gone with the gospel. But there are many difficulties. In some places people are against us. Some places they want to fight and persecute us; but God is with us. And there are places that persecuted very badly before that now have many Christians."

Sergie takes the group to a few of those places. At another community there is a church with the only known Uighur pastor in Uzbekistan. (Uighurs are a mostly unevangelized group centered in and near China.) This man is a study in God's transformational power.

"I came to God through my wife," he tells the group. "She came to God in 1992, and it was very hard for her because I was a communist and director of a huge factory. For 70 years people kept telling us that there is no God."

He threatened her physically. "I was a very cruel man," he says.

He was also an alcoholic. His wife persisted in her faith, and when it seemed her husband was dying of his alcoholism, she brought Christians to the house. He gruffly allowed them to pray for him, and he was healed, and then delivered from alcoholism. He came to Christ, and now the once-abusive alcoholic atheist pastors a thriving church.

At the service, the diverse ethnic makeup is evident. Believers from 12 nationalities call this church home. At the conclusion, four people come to the front and repeat the sinner's prayer before the entire congregation. Once rare in this part of the world, people accepting Christ as their Savior has become a regular occurrence in Central Eurasia.

Worshipping in a location close to a mosque, this congregation has reached out to the Muslim community and won the right to be heard, which results in salvations like tonight's. All four who were saved are Uzbeks.

The next destination is Samarkand, with several stops at new churches along the way.

Cotton fields make regular appearances in the landscape. A major industry, cotton is even part of the national emblem. As we drive, flocks of migratory birds are everywhere. Cattle, sheep and goats populate the valleys, and donkeys are often seen tethered near the roads.

On the banks of the Chirchiq River a young man with a cane pole has caught several fish. In the nearby village, children are on their way to school. Schools function six days a week in Uzbekistan. Christians have touched this village by bringing in a team of doctors to provide free medical care.

Our next destination is a campground alive with activity. Workers labor to improve the facilities on the commodious grounds. The property is a distinct blessing to the many believers who will use it for seminars, retreats, children's camps and more.

At another village there is a small church plant. Few believed in Christ here. Then God healed an unbeliever of cancer. "She ran around the city telling everybody what

Jesus did," the pastor says. And a church was born.

The group passes through areas that are primarily Tajik and Kazakh. A Kazakh graduate of Silk Road Bible College pastors many small Kazakh groups in this area.

At another church, a room is set with decorations and refreshments in preparation for unbelievers who will come for the church's Alpha Course, a low-key evangelism approach. The pastor also has a vision to open a Teen Challenge center in the city, which has the largest concentration of drug addicts and AIDS victims in Uzbekistan.

On the way to the next church, the vehicle Sergie is driving has a blowout. The country's rugged, potholed roads test vehicles to the extreme. And Bishop Sergie tests them as well . . . since he is constantly on the road either in evangelism or support of church plants. The Lord protects those in the car, who change the tire and soon are at the next church, where, like so many of the churches, construction is in progress.

Samarkand

Samarkand is the oldest existing city in Central Eurasia—many think in the whole world. In the old quarter of Samarkand is the Registan, the ancient city square, with some of the most stunning architecture in the world. The square is dominated by the mausoleum of Timur, the cruel conqueror who, in the early 15th century, controlled and ravaged most of Central Eurasia for the Mongol Empire.

In rebuilding Samarkand as his capital, Timur (also known as Tamerlane) made it into the showplace of the East. The splendor still found in Samarkand is a reminder of the cruel despot who nearly obliterated Christianity from the region. Because of this, the move of God here today is all the more remarkable.

The church in Samarkand is distinctive, both for the flawless masonry of its building and the ethnic makeup of its congregation. The majority of the people are Iranian in descent with a unique mix of Iranian and Uzbek culture. Their lilting music forms are unique and compelling.

In 1996 the simple house church in Samarkand had only five or six people. Then God began to move. Many became believers and catapulted the congregation to registered status by 1998.

At the conclusion of the early service, three Iranians— two women and a man—give their hearts to Christ.

The second service is conducted in Uzbek. Following

the message, 27 people stream forward in response to the altar call for salvation. Later, Mark Hausfeld put this remarkable harvest in perspective. "You have seen more Muslims saved today," he point outs to the group, "than many missionaries see in a lifetime of ministry."

It truly is an incredible feeling. Not long ago six pastors in the area were jailed on trumped-up charges. Today . . . revival.

The Iranian pastor, Kahor, had known the Lord for only two years when Sergie talked to him about ministry to Tajiks—a burden that had been on Sergie's heart. Fluent in Russian, Uzbek and Tajik, Kahor has a fulfilling ministry in the multifaceted ethnicity that is Samarkand.

The story of the church along the Silk Road is a story of remarkable individuals, empowered by the Holy Spirit and used by God. There are few as remarkable as Bishop Sergie, and the church in Uzbekistan models vibrant New Testament-style church planting in strategic pioneer places along Central Eurasia's Silk Road.

The Registan in Samarkand

Uzbek dried goods vendor

Uzbek market apples

Samarkand

Tajik children

7

TAJIKISTAN, RIPE FOR HARVEST

*By Taylor Allen**

Blessing

His name means "blessing" in Tajik, the national language of Tajikistan. He is the oldest son of a Muslim family from a small village north of the capital city, Dushanbe. We met him a year or so after arriving in Tajikistan as new "workers." We learned that he was a very ambitious young man who desired more of a life than what the village had to offer. So, he would make frequent trips from his village to our city hoping to meet foreigners, practice his English, and hopefully find work. Other "worker" friends of ours were introduced to "Blessing" as well. We now realize that these were divine appointments as God was lining things up for this young man.

Blessing also received an invitation to the International Fellowship in Dushanbe, Tajikistan, where services are conducted in English. He enjoyed meeting other English speakers and trying to understand everything that was happening. Over a span of several years, we had conversations with him. He would often visit us in our home, usually knocking on our door at a time when we were "busy" with other things and didn't want to be interrupted. In Tajik culture, it can be offensive to turn someone away who arrives at your door unannounced. Traditionally, Tajiks believe that an unexpected visitor is sent from God. "My brother, respect your brother, because the guest comes from God," wrote the 14th-century Tajik poet Hafiz Shirazi. How do you argue with that? So we did our best to provide the hospitality we've come to appreciate so much by serving tea and taking the time to talk and listen. We were just a small part of what God was doing in this young man's life; others in the Christian community were also planting seeds. Was something about to take root and grow?

At times we had difficulty believing anything significant was really happening. He was often angry and cynical. Questions raced through our minds: How far could we go in sharing the gospel to a Muslim like Blessing? Was he sincerely seeking or was he out to get information on us and inform authorities? We went away spiritually and emotionally drained from our conversations, wondering if the investment was worth it, or even too much of a risk.

Upon returning to America for an extended time, we learned from "worker" friends in Tajikistan that Blessing had made a decision to follow Christ. We were thrilled to hear this news but, I must admit, we were skeptical. Could a confused and angry Blessing have a life-transforming experience with Jesus Christ? The pressure to conform to family's and society's expectations in Tajik culture is so great. Could Blessing really have broken away from the norm? I would not make any judgments now. I would wait until our return to Tajikistan.

Ten months later, our paths crossed shortly after our return to Tajikistan. From the moment I saw Blessing I knew he was a new creature in Christ. The anger and cynicism that had once plagued his countenance were gone. They had been replaced by a smile and an attitude that revealed true joy. The promised blessing of Abraham had indeed come to Blessing.

Oh, the blood of Jesus! Even the high, remote mountains of Tajikistan have witnessed its power to save and heal. We sing, "It reaches to the highest mountain . . . ," and I'm reminded of Blessing and how the blood of Jesus has been applied to his heart. There are no barriers, no limits to the grace of God.

South of Tajikistan and across the border is neighboring Afghanistan. My friend Blessing now understands that this gospel is for everyone, even his Muslim Tajik neighbors in Afghanistan. He also realizes that he has been commanded and commissioned by our Lord to "go and make disciples." He has already made several trips into Northern Afghanistan building relationships while doing compassion ministry. And when God opens a door, Blessing is ready to be sent by the church in Tajikistan to live and serve full time among the peoples of Afghanistan. Once again, I'm reminded of the blood of Jesus, how "it flows to the lowest valley." Out of the mountains of Tajikistan and into the lower regions of Afghanistan . . . the blood knows no boundaries.

A Rooftop Experience

It was the Sunday following the 9/11/01 terrorist attack on America and I was in Tajikistan. The world's attention was focused on the situation in Afghanistan, particularly just across the border in northern Afghanistan. U.S. forces had begun bombing there. Our future as "workers" in Tajikistan was uncertain. Were we too close to all the fighting? Would we need to evacuate? In the midst of these questions we tried to maintain some degree of normalcy in our lives. That is why we were, as usual, attending worship at a small local fellowship, trying not to think too hard about the situation to our south.

During the service a young man named Ahmed*, who lives next door to the fellowship, was working on the roof of his house while the believers gathered for worship. While the Spirit worked in our midst, He was also working on the roof of that house in this man's heart. After the meeting Ahmed approached our pastor and explained how God had been working in his life. He had been under conviction for quite some time and felt the need to repent and give his life to Christ. This began a series of conversations as he struggled to make his decision. Ahmed began to attend the meetings as well, observing from the back of the room. In a meeting several weeks later the Tajik pastor concluded his message on the topic of decisions. He called Ahmed forward and announced that he had said yes to Christ. He became the fourth person in his family to make a decision for Christ. His mother and two sisters had been praying for him as well as his father. As Ahmed's father witnesses miracle after miracle in his own home, I have to believe it's not long before the whole family is serving God.

Think about it . . . while the world is focused on the crisis of the hour, while bomb blasts can be heard across the border in Afghanistan, God is directing His love and mercy to one named Ahmed as he works on the roof of his house. Even more incredible than this, He's doing the same thing all over the world, one person at a time. Jesus is determined to get the job done and no crisis will distract

Him from extending His love to the world, one individual at a time. The stories of Blessing and Ahmed testify to this.

Tajikistan is the poorest of the former Soviet Republics and went through a five-year civil war that left thousands dead and the economy devastated. It is 93 percent Muslim. The church of Tajikistan is small in numbers compared to the 6.5 million population. But it is rising to the challenge as God's people are being salt and light in this dark place. Tajikistan is ripe for an unprecedented harvest, one valuable soul at a time.

Tajik mother and daughter

Young men at
Dushanbe market

Tajik elder

Statue of Ismo
Somoni, legend
12th-century
Tajik leader

Tajik children
carrying wood

Dushanbe market vendor

Tajik girl

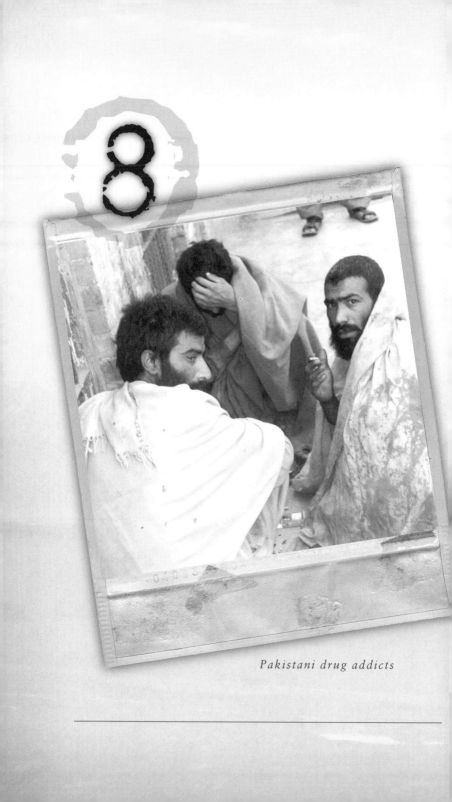

8

Pakistani drug addicts

Chapter Eight

A TREE FOR ADDICTS
By Mark Hausfeld

When God first nudged our hearts about service in Pakistan, our minds needed a jumpstart. In 1991 we knew where Pakistan was, and we knew it was a Muslim country. We knew a bit about the national dress, and we had heard a few exotic stories about life in tribal areas. We were sure that living in Pakistan would not be a ride on a magic carpet, and we didn't know much else.

We certainly didn't know anything about how we might serve in Pakistan. God used some random research in a community library to nudge our hearts a second time. The periodical section we visited relinquished statistics telling us that in a country of roughly 140 million citizens, 7 to 10 million men were heroin addicts. At that moment we knew that God would somehow use us in outreach to those one in seven to 10 Pakistani men. With that assurance in our hearts, and with not much else besides confidence in a God that would prod us toward each next step, my wife, three children and I arrived in Pakistan in the summer of 1995.

Two days after we arrived in Pakistan, we were all enrolled in school; the children were easing into their elementary school setting, and Lynda and I were learning a new script and new sounds in a government language institute. By semester's end Lynda had scored highly in a speech competition, and our female teachers, who took great pleasure in publicly acknowledging that her progress was better than mine, at least had the decency to credit her success to past language experience! Lynda's first language is English, but she grew up in a Spanish-speaking country.

The international school where the children attended learned Lynda was certified to teach Spanish, and they asked her to interview for a job opening they had. Initially we declined, because we were committed to our own Urdu language study. Since Spanish teachers aren't a commodity in Pakistan, the school courted Lynda with the position for a second year. It seemed unlikely that God would place us in Pakistan for Lynda to teach Spanish, but ultimately, we felt God leading her to take the job. She continued Urdu lessons with a tutor, and I remained a full-time student at the language school.

Lynda became friends with a colleague in her new

workplace. Mary* was a Westerner, married to a Pakistani doctor she had fallen in love with in a European university. Early in their friendship, Mary recognized that there must be more to our plans than for Lynda to teach Spanish and for me to be a full-time Urdu student in Pakistan. "So . . . Lynda, what are your long-term reasons for being here?" she asked one day, with a sincere desire to know.

Lynda told her we hoped to establish a drug rehabilitation program in Pakistan. "Your husband and mine ought to get together," she mused out loud. "He has personal interest in seeing drug addicts reached here."

Several weeks into the school year, Lynda and I attended a faculty event. We were making new acquaintances when I noticed that Mary and her husband were looking at me and conversing to one another. Dr. Ali* walked toward me and greeted me in his tribal language. "I'm sorry," I confessed. "I don't understand you." In very fluent English he affably explained that he spoke to me in his native tongue because I looked like I could be from his tribe. He went on to say that Mary had spoken to him of me. "I understand you want to start a drug rehabilitation program in Pakistan." We talked a bit more about Pakistan's great need for such a program, and he said he would like another opportunity to discuss this further.

Six months later, I was taking advantage of a recess from morning language classes to read our city's English newspaper. I recognized Dr. Ali's picture on page four, and read in the article below it that he had just been promoted to the position equivalent to that of Surgeon General in the United States. In my short visit with Dr. Ali those six months earlier, his kindness to me had prompted me to think that I would be privileged to have a friend like him in Pakistan. I wanted to congratulate him. I would speak with Mary first.

"*Mubarak ho!* (Congratulations!)" I announced as she acknowledged my arrival to her office at the school where she and Lynda worked. Mary was politely very proud of her husband. She told me that though Dr. Ali was a renowned surgeon in Pakistan, neither of them ever expected he would be appointed to such a role. She also assured me that her husband was eager to speak with me about Teen Challenge in Pakistan. "If my husband said he wants to talk to you, he means it. If I were you, I would phone him now before he gets too busy." She generously gave me a phone number that would grant me direct access to him in his office.

I drove home and dialed Dr. Ali's number without allowing myself the luxury of much forethought, knowing it was possible I might talk myself out of calling this man who had suddenly become very important. I was nervous, and while the phone rang, my heart pounded.

Dr. Ali's voice on the phone interrupted my angst. "*Asalam-o-aleikum* (God's peace be upon you)," he greeted.

I returned greeting with "*Vo-aleikum-a-salam* (And also with you)." I congratulated him on his new appointment, and we spoke a bit about what this promotion meant to him and to the people of Pakistan. I mustered the courage to remind him that he had expressed interest in further discussion about Teen Challenge in Pakistan. He immediately asked if we might be able to arrange a high level meeting about the matter. He explained that I would need to invite a representative from the Global Teen Challenge headquarters to Pakistan for discussions. We discussed this meeting a bit further, and parted with expectation of future collaboration.

Global Teen Challenge's emissary was Jesse Owen, whose winsome personality was perfect for this meeting. After tea and a delightful visit, Dr. Ali steered the conversation in the direction of our hopes for Teen Challenge in Pakistan. "We are here to discuss Teen Challenge," he said, "but before we do, I want to say something."

Dr. Ali looked us in the eyes and said, "I don't believe

psychology, counseling or therapies alone are the answer to seeing drug addicts set free from addictions." I wondered if what I felt in the pit of my stomach was forewarning that Dr. Ali was about to deliver difficult stipulations.

Dr. Ali continued. "I believe the only way for a drug addict to be set free from drugs is through a relationship with God."

I probably sighed audibly. Jesse and I assured Dr. Ali that the focus of Teen Challenge is exactly that. We explained to him how faith in God, prayer, and devotion to the Holy Scriptures are foundational to the program's methods of drug rehabilitation. The Holy Spirit was palpable in our midst. At the end of our meeting Dr. Ali said something I will never forget. "Mark and Jesse, today we have put our hands together and planted a seed in the soil of Pakistan that is going to grow into a beautiful tree and provide shade and rest for the drug addicts of this country."

Seven months after our meeting, the government of the Islamic Republic of Pakistan hosted a signing ceremony, officially granting Teen Challenge Pakistan the registration that would enable this outreach to drug addicts of that great nation.

Years have passed, and Teen Challenge Pakistan continues to touch men who have been decimated by drug use. The lives of the graduates testify to the effectiveness of the program. Their families and communities see the change that the Truth of God brings into a person's life.

Recently, following his program graduation ceremony, one such recovering addict came to me and said, "Dr. Mark, I feel that I am under a tree that provides me shade and rest." Dr. Ali was right—prophetic in a sense that we all appreciate more than he knows. Teen Challenge Pakistan offers rest and recovery to the hopeless addict, and because of the Calvary tree, points him toward restoration and new life.

Wheat harvesters near a Teen
Challenge Center in Pakistan

Graduation
celebration at the
Attock Teen
Challenge

Pastor Mehdi Dibaj (left) and Bishop Haik Hovsepian, Iranian Assemblies of God martyrs

9

IRAN: CROWNS OF THE MARTYRS

By Lynda Hausfeld

Today I watched the videotaped memorial service of an Iranian martyr. I first heard the news of his death in his homeland 11 years ago from my Chicago hospital bed. I was recovering from surgery, but I recall the deep sadness I felt then at the thought of his family's pain and the fact of a church's loss. I resented my own neatly bandaged wounds; they were meaningless compared to his. I was incised painlessly in a sanitized operating room; tidy stitches and crisp, white bandages would ensure a swift and comfortable recovery. Bishop Haik Hovsepian Mehr was stabbed repeatedly in the chest. One can only presume the violence and terror of that moment. His hastily buried body was exhumed 10 days later, when his family finally learned the reason for his disappearance.

The video of this Westminster Central Hall, London memorial service flashes onscreen to an exhilarating choral rendition of Handel's "Messiah." Haik's life would be remembered for the act of worship it was. He planted churches and pastored leaders. As chairman of the Council of Pastors of the Iranian Protestant Churches he fostered collaboration and unity among all denominations in Iran. Dignitaries and interdenominational church officials attended Haik's funeral as witness to this man's influence and the impact he had on hosts of believers and secular leaders worldwide. Those present knew that Haik was the real deal. He knew the cost of discipleship, and his love for God and his fellowman drove him to pay the dearest price.

Sam Yeghnazar, then senior pastor of the Iranian Christian Fellowship, memorialized Haik's "real-deal" life in the service. Interestingly, Sam himself comes from pioneer stock, since his father was responsible for planting a house church which later became the Assemblies of God Church in Iran. Sam tells the story of how his father, a man of prayer and the Word, became convinced over time that the baptism in the Holy Spirit was for him. After a long time of seeking and prayer, God met this servant in his workplace and baptized him with His Holy Spirit.

He had waited for years for this experience and he tried to keep it secret for the fear he might lose it. However, after nine days he could not keep it secret any longer. Early in the morning he woke up his wife and all six children with this message: "If Jesus were to return today, are you ready to meet Him?" All the family sought the Lord with tears and soon everyone was speaking in other tongues. With the help of a family friend who joined the Yeghnazar family prayer meetings, the Assemblies of God of Iran was started.

There would be a price to pay for church growth in Iran. In the early 1970s a Norwegian evangelist prophesied that difficulties lay ahead. Then tragedy struck. Haik and Takoosh Hovsepian, along with their young son, were riding home from a meeting outside Tehran with Assemblies of God missionaries Mark and Gladys Bliss and their three children. It was very dark, and Mark did not see the slowly moving farm vehicle driving ahead of him with its lights off. At the same time an oncoming vehicle had its high beams on.

The Bliss vehicle hit the nearly invisible farm truck. In the hospital both couples learned that all of their children had died in the accident. Gladys and the Hovsepians were injured, as well. Ruth Clark, who with her husband served as facilitator for missionaries and the work in Iran, recalled, "Mark later told me that Haik kept his guitar under his hospital bed. When he and Takoosh would feel a wave of grief, Haik would pull out his guitar and begin singing hymns—and they would bring comfort not only to their room, but to Mark and Gladys' room nearby."

Sam Yeghnazar recalled this sorrowful event at Brother Haik's memorial. Mark Bliss was sitting on the large platform, just a few rows behind the pulpit. I recognized Mark in the video, and thanked God for giving him and Gladys to Iran. To this day this couple continues to serve Iran, though they are well into retirement years and have not been able to return there since the revolution. Many people continue to be strengthened by their courage and lasting love for Iran and for Muslims in that great country.

Before the accident, the Blisses had begun meeting with three other missionary couples for times of prayer. Within the remainder of that year, the three other missionary couples had each lost at least one child as well. The price being paid was steep, and many were paying it.

As if serving Christ were not already proving costly, the revolution of 1979 brought immense change to Iran and to the church. The Ayatollah Khomeini declared Iran a new Islamic republic in February 1979. The core of his reform would be the Islamization of a society that had liberally westernized under the Shah's rule.

Government intruded into matters of church life and existence. Property rights were modified, which forced church closures. Properties held by the Episcopal Church of Iran were confiscated. The Bible Society of Iran was closed and remains closed to this day. The persecution of

Christians, especially those of Muslim background, began in earnest.

In 1979 Mehdi Dibaj, a Muslim-background Assemblies of God pastor who loved Muslims and shared his faith unreservedly with them, was incarcerated for his faith. He was released after 68 days, but was re-arrested in 1984.

While Mehdi Dibaj was in prison, another Muslim-background Assemblies of God pastor, Hossein Soodman, lost his Mashad parish to government church closures. In September of 1990 he took a pastorate in another city. He was arrested immediately, interrogated, released, and forced to return to Mashad. There he was again taken into custody, and was tortured for his faith. After one more release he was re-imprisoned, and on December 3, 1990, was hanged in prison for his conversion from Islam and his work as a church leader.

Three years later, Mehdi was still in prison. Following a total of nine years in captivity, where he suffered repeated beatings, two years of solitary confinement, and mock executions, Mehdi was charged with apostasy and sentenced to death. Mehdi didn't fear this end, and he didn't resent his unjust incarceration. In his own written defense delivered to the Sari Court of Justice in December 1993, he proclaimed, "I am filled to overflowing with joy; I am not only satisfied to be in prison . . . but I am ready to give my life for the sake of Jesus Christ."

Haik Hovsepian, then bishop of the Assemblies of God in Iran and chairman of the Council of Pastors of the Iranian Protestant Churches, refused to relinquish this servant quietly. "If we go to jail or die for our faith, we want the whole Christian world to know what has happened to their brothers and sisters." He shook the world with news of Dibaj's death sentence, and the world reacted. On January 16, 1994, due to international pressure that resulted from Haik's efforts, Iran's government released its prisoner.

Three days later, Haik Hovsepian Mehr failed to return from a routine run to the airport. On January 30, 1994, after two weeks of repeatedly denying they knew the whereabouts of a man they had kept under surveillance 24 hours a day, government representatives exhumed Haik's body from a Muslim cemetery and released it to his family for Christian burial in Tehran. Standing over the grave of the man who had saved his life, Mehdi Dibaj lamented, "You stole my martyr's crown."

Haik wouldn't be the last of Iran's martyrs. Though authorities released Mehdi Dibaj from prison, his death sentence remained intact. Five months following his release, he mysteriously disappeared and was found murdered.

Tateos Michaelean, who replaced Haik as chairman of the Council of Pastors of the Iranian Protestant Churches, disappeared on June 29, 1994. His dismembered body was reportedly found in a freezer. He died from bullet wounds to the head.

Assemblies of God pastor Muhammad Bagher Yusefi, guardian of Mehdi's sons during his imprisonment, left early one morning to spend some time in prayer. His body was found hanging from a tree in a forest not far from his home on September 28, 1996.

Today Hamid Pourmand, another Assemblies of God leader in Iran, sits in prison waiting to be tried for apostasy. At this writing, it could happen any day. In Islamic court, it's a crime punishable by death.

Those of us whose place it is to watch and pray for the Iranian church remain challenged by this extraordinary band of believers to a life of re-defined grace and purpose. The gift of eternal life is free, but it's costly . . . especially when we share it.

Post-script

As *Silk Road Stories* was being completed, there was a significant development in Iran. We sent the following communiqué:

Dear Family and Friend of Missions,

We have just received word, which has been verified by our Iranian liaisons, that Hamid Pourmand has been acquitted of the charge of apostasy! This is very good news, indeed! In Iran, apostasy is a crime punishable by death.

Hamid has been returned from his hometown where he stood trial, to prison in Tehran. He will continue to be held on his previous conviction, including charges of espionage. Hamid was convicted of failure to inform his military officials of his Christian beliefs, in spite of proof Hamid presented to the contrary.

We are thrilled to impart good news, but sobered by the need to continue praying. According to sources in Iran, Hamid is safer in Tehran. While we rejoice over the recent acquittal, we now need to pray for his continued safety. If he were to be released, he would be vulnerable to assassination attempts. Since 1990 four Assemblies of God ministers in Iran have been found dead following "disappearances" and evidence of brutal murder. One of those, Mehdi Dibaj, was killed following his release from prison, which was largely due to international pressure and protest against his sentence to death for apostasy.

Thank you for interceding on behalf of the Pourmands and the Iranian national church during this difficult time. God is showing himself faithful and powerful to all of us, for the Glory of His kingdom.

Together for the harvest,

Mark and Lynda Hausfeld
AGWM Area Director Office
Central Eurasia

*Bam, Iran, earthquake damage; Assemblies
of God workers provided relief*

*Hamid Pourmand
and family*

Mir Muhammad in the kitchen

Chapter Ten

MIR MUHAMMAD: A MUSLIM TO THE MUSLIMS

By Lydia Cyrus *

I met Mir Muhammad during the arduous six-month process of house hunting for a location for a business that I was planning to open in the capital city of Pakistan. He was the *chowkidar*—or guard—for a retired general who owned the house. But, unlike most *chowkidars*, he was not sitting idly around the gate but was very actively involved with all the renovations that were taking place.

He welcomed my friend and me into the house and proudly showed us every nook and cranny, as we stepped over piles of wood, walked over unfinished floors past busy workmen, and carefully avoided cans of paint. I loved the house. It was perfect for the business I was going to open.

Over the next month I negotiated with the owner, who in the end decided to rent the house to the other interested tenants. Disappointed, I started my search again.

Just when I had almost given up hope of finding a suitable location, I found another house. Even though this house needed lots of work it had great potential. I needed to hire a guard.

One day, I noticed Mir Muhammad walking along the street and I stopped to talk with him. He said that the new people had moved into the general's house and hired another guard so he no longer had his job. I told him I needed a guard and asked if he would like to interview for this job.

This posed a problem for me. A single woman in the Muslim world lives with many restrictions. A woman's reputation is extremely important and most women are not allowed to live alone. I needed to be sure that whomever I hired was a good man. I sensed that God wanted me to hire Mir Muhammad.

Mir Muhammad, a refugee from Kashmir in his mid-40s, had 10 children. He and his family had been uprooted and had lost everything. His wife and the youngest eight of their 10 children now lived with Mir Muhammad's parents just five miles from the Line of Control between Pakistan and Kashmir. Sporadic gun fights break out constantly in their area. Like many men from that area, he left the village to find work in the city. He lived in the city and was only able to return home for 10 days every two months. His wife was left with the responsibility of raising the children while he earned money to bring back to them.

Had this trustworthy, shrewd businessman been born in a different place and time he could have been an executive of a major company. He was gifted, industrious and intelligent.

Mir Muhammad was a devout Muslim . . . the most devout I have ever met. He prayed faithfully five times a day. Before the morning call to prayer, well before sunrise, he would get up and chant the Koran in his room for two hours. During the month of Ramazan, when Muslims fast from sunrise to sunset for 30 days, Mir Muhammad would often fast for 40 days. He was a "Muslim to the Muslims," just as Paul was a "Hebrew to the Hebrews." I sincerely prayed that one day he would be the next apostle Paul for South Asia.

I was challenged by his devotion and dedication to what he believed. So devoted was Mir Muhammad that he painstakingly wrote out the Koran by hand in such beautiful calligraphy that not even a computer could reproduce it—one copy for himself and one copy for his father. Yet my heart grieved that he only knew Jesus as a prophet. He had such a zeal for God but in all his efforts to please Him, he did not know if he would go to heaven or not.

We had many discussions over the years that he worked for me. He commented on how our Christian customers treated him with respect.

The other guards in our neighborhood gave him the honored title of "Sufi." They recognized his devotion to Allah. One winter night around Christmastime at about 11:30 the doorbell rang and I looked out of the window to see Mir Muhammad disappear into the small shacks at the vacant property next door where a very poor family were living as caretakers. He was there for quite a while. I was concerned that maybe someone was sick and needed a ride to the hospital.

I got dressed and went down to ask if everything was all right. He said that a baby had just been born and they had called him to speak the creed "There is no god but Allah and Muhammad is his prophet" into the baby's ear. Islam requires that every Muslim baby must hear those words first. I asked if I could go and see the baby. By the light of the moon I entered the smoke-filled shack and saw the newborn baby girl wrapped in blankets. Her tired young mother was curled up on some dirty blankets in a corner.

She was disappointed that her baby was a girl.

A girl baby is considered a burden and a huge responsibility. From the time she is born, parents worry about providing a dowry for her. They are concerned with protecting her, for if anything happens to her the family honor is at stake.

Sons, on the other hand, are welcomed with great joy because they will provide for their parents in their old age and carry on the family name. In the extended family, sons live with their wives and children in the home of their parents. Girls leave their homes to join their husbands' families. Mir Muhammad had those concerns for his daughters.

After I left the country I heard that Mir Muhammad had died from asphyxiation when the gas heater in his room had gone out during the night. He had just returned from visiting his family one last time.

I grieved for his wife and family. I grieved for the shortness of his life. I grieved with the realization that, even though Mir Muhammad was a good man, his goodness could not bring him salvation. The unanswered question plagued my heart: Had Mir Muhammad met Jesus Christ, the One who is the way, the truth and the life?

Chiltrali man

Chiltrali musicians

Kalash girl

Azerbaijani mosque

Chapter Eleven

"SAVE THE SINNER"
*As told to David Murphy**

My name is Farhadov Jhun. I was born in Baku, Azerbaijan, in 1962. I was born into a well-educated family. My father is an engineer and my mother, a doctor. I have a brother who is two years younger than I. My family was very serious; however, I always knew that my parents loved me. Growing up I loved boxing and was good enough to be a member of the Azerbaijani boxing team. After my boxing career I went on to study at the Sport University.

Growing up in a Communist country we were not told much about God. What little we did hear was anti-God. We were taught that our goal was communism and that there was no God. Communism taught us to think about life now and not to focus on life after death. Still, I knew in my heart that there was a God. I had heard my parents and grandparents talk about God, but I never thought about Him personally. My idea was that He was an old man that sat up in heaven and controlled everyone. I was not afraid of death. I believed that after you died someone would bury you and that was it. I did believe if somehow there really was an afterlife I would go to heaven. Twice in my early life I had had close encounters with death. Once I almost drowned in a lake. The second time I was run over by a car and survived. If there was a God, it seemed He was pleased with me and was protecting me.

I also loved to read fantasy books about good and evil, heaven and hell, as well as science books and magazines. As I read these I began to wonder who created the world and all the things in it.

The only time that I heard about Christianity was around Christmastime. I believed that Muhammad was the prophet of the Muslims and that Jesus was the prophet of the Christians. Over time I became more religious and began to call on Allah, Muhammad and Ali (the cousin and son-in-law of Muhammad). At this time I didn't think I was a sinner. I believed that I was a good person. To me sinners were murderers, thieves and immoral people. Around 1994 I began to think more and more about my soul and the purpose of life. The more I thought about the lack of purpose in life the more depressed I became. At one point I became so depressed that I asked myself, *why live?* My disillusionment led me into a life of smoking, drinking and drugs.

In 1994 I was working in a store when a customer began
to witness to me. She told me that I was a sinner and
invited me to church. I went, and my first time there, I saw
people whose faces were glowing. I liked going to church
and enjoyed the preaching. Many times I would cry as
I listened to the sermons. I began to realize that I was a
sinner. There were so many people at the meetings that I
had to stand at the door, however many times I felt that
the pastor was speaking to me and that he knew my life.

On October 29, 1994, I gave my life to Jesus. Even
though I repented of my sins I didn't understand
everything that I was doing. I continued to smoke, drink
and do drugs for the next five days. On November 4th my
brother and I and three of our friends decided to smoke
marijuana. It would be the last day I ever smoked.

There was just a small amount and it should not have
affected us. But 30 minutes after smoking I began to feel
that I was dying. I felt I saw my soul leave my body and
heard Jesus say, "Only death can pay for your sins." I saw
the angel of death coming for me and I began to scream.
My brother and his friends tried to quiet me but could
not. After a few minutes I saw my dead body, the room I
was in and my brother and our friends. The next things
that I saw I cannot adequately express with words. I saw
people burning in hell; there was fire, suffering, fear and
darkness everywhere. I saw a large door, in front of which

was a huge demon with two horns and big teeth.

Then two angels, dressed completely in white, with white hair and wings, came and took me to heaven. Everything was bright and shiny; even the sun shone differently. The light was brighter than anything I had ever seen before. The angels took me back and forth from heaven to hell four times. The fourth time they took me from hell they took me to a place where I could see a large city. In the city there were men, women, children, old people and young people. Everyone was wearing white and all of them were singing, worshipping, dancing and rejoicing. Above the city there were two chariots; they were on fire. God was in the fire but I could not see His face. He turned to me and spoke in a language that I had not learned but yet I understood. He offered me salvation; I thought that I was going to stay in heaven. But my spirit returned to my body. Two and a half hours after I had died my spirit came back to my body and I began to breathe again.

The entire time I was in hell I could hear the same thing over and over again. Someone was praying for me and kept saying, "Save the sinner, save the sinner, save the sinner."

At first I was afraid, but as I continued to go to church and tell Christians about my experience I began to feel more and more at peace. Shortly after this my brother and mother-in-law were saved. I continued to tell my story and began to preach. On March 12, 1995, I was baptized with my wife and her mother and brothers.

Later I was filled with the Holy Spirit. In 1997 I started Living Stones Church. I have seen many miracles since then. I have seen people saved, healed and set free. Today my entire family serves the Lord and they help me in the church. We need our brothers and sisters to pray for us and for the people of Azerbaijan. There are only a few thousand believers in our country of 8 million. We need the prayers of believers all around the world. Your prayers will help us to reach our country for Jesus. Please pray that God would "save the sinner," just like I believe someone was praying for me.

Baku shipyard

Azerbaijani woman with cell phone

Turkish carpet weaver

12

A MIRACULOUS INTERVENTION IN ISTANBUL

By Troy Caye*

This is a story of how Jesus Christ reached into the broken lives of twin brother and sister Erhan and Esra*. They grew up in the largest city in Turkey, in a fairly large Muslim family with five children, which is common for families in the city of Istanbul. There are over 15 million people living now in this metropolis, which is more than one-fifth of the whole country's population. Although their family had enough money to live on, they were simple, working-class people. Having at least a primary school education would help the twins get a job and earn some money to help support the family. Oftentimes, grown children stay in their parents' home until they are married, so while they are single they still can contribute to running the household.

Both Erhan and Esra had had unfortunate life-changing experiences. Esra was hit by a car as a teenager; she struggled with side effects which affected her thinking processes. She was quite lonely, and had few friends, though she had a deep friendship with her twin brother, Erhan.

Erhan had lost a close friend in an untimely death and his grief caused him to give up on life—even to stop learning to play the guitar, though he had a great love for music. He struggled with low self-esteem, and eventually turned to drugs and alcohol as a way to deal with his inner turmoil.

Then Jesus, in His great mercy, stepped into their lives, first by revealing himself to Esra. In a dream, she saw Jesus in all His brilliance sitting before her. He had white hair, white clothes, and tender eyes. His brightness illuminated her dark world as Jesus himself began to reveal His loving care for her. In her mind's eye she saw her head resting on His lap as Jesus was caressing her hair. This act spoke deeply to her, communicating His love for her. He said, "It's OK to believe in Me." She then awoke with such peace and joy as she had never known before, knowing that it was Jesus who was calling her to seek and find Him more.

She wanted to find a church in Istanbul; God had miraculously arranged the situation. In the next apartment building light had been shining for a few years. Three different foreign Christian families had at different times taken up residence there. And now a new neighbor for Esra had arrived, a single German Christian worker who was attending our fellowship. Esra assumed that because this woman was not Turkish, she must be a Christian. Esra, who did not know this foreigner but had often observed her, asked her to take her along to a church meeting. Esra happily attended worship times, the first one a special Easter celebration with dinner. After a few short weeks, she personally accepted the love of Christ and chose to follow Him.

Esra began studying the Bible with other women and developed a burden for evangelism and prayer. She began to pray for her twin brother and asked us to join with her in doing so, knowing that only Jesus could help him get his life sorted out. Erhan had not been able to hold down a job due to his addictions. Therefore, his father had kicked him out of the house. But Esra longed to share her newfound faith with her dear brother whom she hadn't seen for a time. Without any place to live, he had been sleeping along the Marmara seafront in our part of the city.

One balmy June evening, less than two months after Esra had come to the Lord, Erhan was sitting on a park bench when he saw a vision of Jesus. Jesus reached out His nail-pierced hands toward him and spoke peace to his heart, telling him to go home to make things right. On his walk home through the busy pedestrian shopping street, he saw an old Armenian church. He decided to enter a church building for the first time in his life. Inside he lit a candle as a token of his response of reaching out to Jesus. Somehow he knew that Christianity had something to do with his recent vision.

When he arrived home, Esra was overjoyed to see that Jesus had answered her prayers. She immediately shared her newfound faith, pulling out her copy of the newly translated New Testament in modern Turkish and sharing a verse with him. She invited him to come to our Sunday church meeting the next day. He agreed.

They walked together to our home where, outside our apartment building, she introduced us. We were a bit apprehensive of what our neighbors would think (they always know what you are doing and whom you are with). Erhan didn't look like your typical well-groomed Turkish man. He was dressed completely in black with long, stringy black hair and a very blank look in his eyes. In short, it was obvious that he was a drug addict.

Our two young children immediately loved him. Despite his outward appearance, they accepted him for who he was. He felt very loved as he joined the worship time. That same day, following the meeting, we had a special time of prayer for him in a side room and he accepted the Lord. He was immediately set free from his addictions. We saw the Lord working powerfully in his life.

After nearly 10 years, he is still a faithful core member of our fellowship. He has studied the Word much and grown in his faith. He also has a very special ministry. He visits seekers of Jesus and helps them to establish initial relationships. Esra continued to meet with us over the years but, after marrying, she has moved to the Asian side of the city. (Istanbul is divided into European and Asian sections by the mile-wide Bosporus Strait which connects the Black Sea to the Marmara Sea.) She is still involved in church life, helping to lead a women's group and using her gift of evangelism in a local fellowship. Both Erhan and Esra are Spirit-filled believers growing in the grace of Jesus and blessing the small but growing body of Christ in Turkey. We thank Jesus that He stepped into their lives in this miraculous way and we believe that He will continue to miraculously reveal himself to many other Muslim men and women.

Sights of Istanbul

Faisal Mosque, the world's largest mosque, in Islamabad, Pakistan

Chapter Thirteen

NABIL'S MIRACLE
By Lynda Hausfeld

South Asian food was somewhat new to me, but I liked it. On this particular day, I just couldn't keep it down. My afternoon battle with nausea and fever chills followed a daunting morning of language learning at the university where my husband and I had started our studies. I had made it home without having suffered the humiliation of losing my breakfast in front of my Pakistani instructors, but I had since lost that and more. I was plumb sick.

In the middle of that miserably dizzy, snail's-paced afternoon, the doorbell rang. Mark had afternoon commitments, so I was home alone. It meant the doorbell was mine to answer.

I made my way upstairs through a vortex of spinning walls, and managed to see who was at our house. It was Nabil*, an acquaintance Mark had made at language school. He was a young fellow, about 20, who was

working on his bachelor's degree in English at the institute
where Mark and I were beginning to sputter in Urdu.
I thought for sure that he would take one look at my
infirmed face and run. When he didn't, I volunteered news
of the obvious. "I'm sorry, Nabil. My husband is away,
and I'm not well." I asked if he would like to come later.

He graciously declined my offer and stepped through
the door into our living room. This stunned me for two
reasons. First, Nabil was an unimposing fellow of slight
build and gentle mannerisms. He barely spoke above a
whisper, and I didn't sense he was forcing his way into
our home. But there he was! Second, Nabil and I both
knew that it was highly inappropriate for him, a Muslim
man, to be in the lone company of a female. I had only
been in Pakistan a few weeks, but already had learned the
art of not looking into a man's face when in his company.
I knew the improprieties of touch and presence, and
understood that if anything were to go awry, I would be
the one society would blame.

I asked the Lord a number of things in the few seconds I
had to decide what I would do next. Actually, I screamed
silently, but so desperately that I still remember the ache
in my throat and chest. "God, what is this man up to?
Doesn't he see that I can't do this right now? Please, just
get him out of here!"

Nabil must have felt as comfortable as I felt awkward, because he settled into the cane sofa's cushions and carried on with impeccably polite conversation and guest behavior. I did my best to keep some semblance of congeniality plastered on my sweaty, pale face, and I must have hidden my bewilderment and frustration well enough. By this time I had realized that most likely due to language barriers, Nabil had probably misunderstood the offer I made him when he first came in, and had not caught on to the fact that I was ill. Nabil seemed pleased to converse with me while he waited for my husband, and since God wasn't removing him, I just went with the flow. Two hours later Mark came through the front door, and his relationship with Nabil began.

Their initial discussions were about just about anything. As Mark and Nabil grew closer in mutual trust and friendship, Nabil assumed a protective role over Mark and our family, counseling us in matters of culture and life in Pakistan. Mark's and Nabil's casual discussions morphed into studies that took them through the Koran and the Holy Scriptures. They were careful never to offend one or the other in their conversations, and they enjoyed one another's company. Over the months, Nabil's interest shifted from wanting to study the Koran and Scriptures with Mark, to wanting to study just the Scriptures. The stories of Jesus and His miracles seemed to interest Nabil the most.

This exchange went on for months. Nabil completed his bachelor's degree and went on to complete his master's in English at a very conservative Islamic university. During this time he had begun attending church with our family, at considerable personal risk to himself. We would meet him at an undisclosed place away from his home and family, take him to church, and drop him off afterwards. Nabil had not yet professed Christ, but he was drawn to Him in a very special way.

One day Mark received a dreadful phone call. Nabil had been struck by a car while riding his bike home from school.

Mark rushed to be with Nabil at the hospital. He learned that Nabil had a fractured skull and a severe concussion, and found him in a ward crowded with patients and guests. Nabil's extended family hovered around his bedside, extremely concerned that the only son of his parents might not survive his injuries. Nabil was thrashing violently in pain.

Mark approached Nabil and simply asked if he could pray for him. Nabil's reply was clear. In front of his Muslim family and the other patients and guests in the ward, Nabil boldly said, "Please pray for me in Jesus' name." Mark did, and quietly promised Nabil he would return to see him the next day.

Mark's love for his friend compelled him to seek the
counsel of an expatriate physician, also a believer, who
agreed to accompany him to the hospital to see Nabil.
Care in this hospital was known to be inferior at times,
and Mark wanted Nabil to have the benefit of a second
evaluation.

He and Dr. Jane approached Nabil's ward, and from
a distance saw that Nabil's entire body was covered in a
sheet. In the West, this would mean that the patient had
expired. In Pakistan, it means the individual wants to be
alone. Dr. Jane politely told the folk present that she was
a physician and would like to see the patient's chart. They
allowed her to proceed.

It was Dr. Jane's turn to be confused. She whispered
to Mark, "It seems they are testing his thyroid, and they
suspect he has colon cancer!" Mark wondered how a head
injury could turn into all this, and asked the family if he
and Dr. Jane might be permitted to see the patient. They
replied, "Why not?" They removed the sheet to reveal a
man in his 50s! Nabil was missing!

Mark and Dr. Jane learned from the nurses' station
that Nabil had been discharged earlier that day. They
immediately made their way to Nabil's home, and
knocked on the door. To their joy and amazement, Nabil
answered and invited them in! Before offering so much as

a greeting, Nabil asked Mark if what he had experienced was the same healing power of Jesus they had talked about in their times together.

"Yes, Nabil," Mark affirmed, "you have experienced the healing power of Jesus Christ. He has touched you!" In typical Pakistani fashion, Nabil graciously offered them a seat, and served them tea and snacks. The doctor, who had herself just witnessed her first miracle as a believer, sipped tea and watched Nabil through wide eyes. Mark's heart was electrified. Though comments were brief and cautious, the miracle was big and careless!

Two months later, Nabil attended a thanksgiving service with us in our church. At the end of the service, the pastor instructed everyone to form circles with close friends and family. Nabil joined hands with Mark, our children, and myself. When the opportunity for public thanksgiving was given, Nabil prayed out loud, with clarity and confidence. "Father, I thank You that I have come to know Jesus Christ."

God worked in Nabil's life like He works in the lives of many Muslims He draws to himself. He honored his seeker heart, and gave him opportunity to learn the Word. Then He confirmed it through personal, miraculous revelation and healing.

Pakistani shoe shine street shop

Open air worship in Rawalpindi

Wheat harvesters in Peshawar

Muslim at prayer

THREE ENCOUNTERS WITH ISA ALONG THE SILK ROAD

By Robert Lee *

Second Corinthians 6: 6, 7 says, "In purity, understanding, patience and kindness; in the Holy Spirit and in sincere love; in truthful speech and in the power of God, with weapons of righteousness in the right hand and in the left." In my 23 years of ministry to Muslims, I have seen many come to faith through three kinds of encounters, all mentioned in the above text.

Truth Encounter

We had lived in Central Asia for four years, in a major city that was relatively westernized, when I felt impressed by the Holy Spirit to move. My wife, three children, and I made the move across the country to a place where our nearest fellowship was 600 miles away. It was a hard place to live and raise a family. The city was in the midst of a bloody ethnic conflict that claimed the lives of thousands, and it was full of displaced peoples living in wretched conditions. For months I had no indication of why God had sent us there.

There was an ancient Orthodox church in the city. But over the centuries, the Christian community had dwindled to a few families among a sea of Muslims. I felt impressed to become active in the church even though its rituals were strange to me—incense, candles, icons, golden-robed priests, and a set liturgy. After the priest and I became friends, he shared with me about Daoud*.

Daoud was a Muslim businessman and a father of many children. He was not devout; drinking and womanizing were his life. Then he went bankrupt. While unemployed, he began to read the Koran over and over. In the Koran he read that there were previous holy books, such as the Tawrat (books of Moses), Injil (the Gospels), and the Zebur (writings of David). He went to the Orthodox church and asked the priest for an Injil. With much fear the priest gave him one. After reading the Injil over and over, Daoud believed in Christ and wanted to be baptized.

Until Daoud, the priest had never even heard of a Muslim reading the Bible, let alone meeting one who wanted to follow Christ and be baptized. He told Daoud that he could not baptize him as it was contrary to church rules to baptize someone from a non-Christian background. For months Daoud was in limbo, but then the priest introduced us. Within a few months other people in the city came to faith and we had the beginnings of a small fellowship. Several of Daoud's children came to faith and the Lord provided him with new work. After months of uncertainty as to why the Lord had led us to this difficult city, we finally saw His purposes.

Recently, after many years, I had a chance to visit the city again. There is now a new church, built and paid for at great sacrifice by the local believers of Muslim background. A lengthy series of court cases eventually won for them the right to meet in their new building where they have substantial freedom to distribute the Scriptures and discuss Christ with inquirers. Teachers often bring their schoolchildren to the church for field trips. It is a true light in a city of great darkness, despair, and poverty. In a city where Islam had replaced Christianity, the Lord is building a new expression of His body among Muslims.

Power Encounter

In another city along the Silk Road, a young man earned his living by doing incredible feats of strength and demonstrations of karate. Nuri* looked much like a Central Asian Arnold Schwarzenegger, with bulging muscles all over his body. Sometimes he would lie on the street beneath a jacked-up truck as it was lowered onto his stomach. For several seconds he would support the entire weight of the truck on his midsection. Perhaps his most daring feat involved resting his Adam's apple on the point of a sword tightly held in a vise on the ground. His partner would then break a club (resembling a baseball bat) over his neck.

All of his muscles, however, could not save Nuri from cancer. When we read about him in a local newspaper, he was 25 years old, and he had been a patient in a hospital for several months. Doctors gave him only a few months to live. My partner and I began to visit him regularly in the hospital, and we gave him an Injil. We learned that he needed several thousand dollars to have an operation in a larger city. We helped raise the money and sent him to the big city hospital. Before he went, however, we prayed for him in Isa's name.

Surprisingly, a few days later, Nuri returned. He was extremely puzzled. Every X-ray had previously shown his body to be full of cancer; all the doctors had said he was dying. Yet now, they said they could find no cancer. They found only a couple of tumors that could easily be removed. Nuri couldn't understand.

We explained to Nuri that Isa (Jesus) is still a Healer, just like He was 2,000 years ago; He was the one who had healed him. To Nuri this seemed impossible. He had a dark side to his past. He had committed murder for hire more than once. "Allah can't forgive murder," he told us.

We shared with him about David and Paul from the Bible, two great men of God who had also committed murder. Nuri was able to accept that it really was Isa that had healed him. Soon the Lord also set him free of the demonic spirits through which many of his feats of strength had been done. This powerful man had experienced a power far greater than any he had known— the power of Isa, Jesus Christ.

Love encounter

Muhammad's life has been a hard one. Born into a Muslim home, he lost his mother at the age of 1. He was raised by uncaring relatives in poor, tough neighborhoods. One day he ordered a Bible that he had seen offered in a newspaper. Muhammad tried to follow Christ, but found he could not overcome his alcoholism and other vices.

I got to know Muhammad and spent many hours with him through some very tough times. Eventually, the Lord totally set him free; now Muhammad is my travel partner for months every summer.

Last summer we followed up on people who came

to faith many years earlier, during our second term, between 1987 and 1991. Many of them had been without fellowship since then. I was astonished at how these believers remembered details of our times together. They remembered few of the messages I had worked so hard to prepare in their language. What they did remember were the meals in my home and the informal times of Christian fellowship—mostly outdoors since we had no place to meet. According to Muhammad, as important as miracles and exposure to the Word of God are, the most effective way to touch a Muslim heart is through relationship that demonstrates the love of Christ.

These three illustrations are representative of many who have met Christ in these ways. There are also many stories that have yet to be told—of people whose encounter with Isa is yet future. Their stories might focus on God's power to heal and deliver, or on the truth of the Word that spoke to their hearts. They may tell a story of how a sincere servant of Christ faithfully and patiently showed them the love of Christ. Let's pray that the Holy Spirit will draw millions more from the lands of the Silk Road into an encounter with the risen Christ.

*Veiled Shiite
Muslim woman*

Buzkashi, Central Asian equivalent of polo

Broom man

Melon vendors at market

Silk Road winter

Afghan naan shop

15

THE AFGHAN FLYING CARPET

By Kathryn Dawn O'Malley *

Today my friend Zarmeena rode a flying carpet. At least that's my summary of what she was telling me. As we sat on the floor in my bedroom drinking tea it reminded me of my first encounter with Zarmeena, who, as of today, is also my sister in Christ.

Zarmeena and I first became acquainted at a farewell for her niece, Zweeta, who had recently obtained refugee status in Pakistan and was headed to Europe. She and her family would join her father, Zarmeena's elder brother, who had been there for almost three years already.

Earlier Zweeta's father had lost all hope for a better Afghanistan. First Soviets invaded their country. Then their own Mujahadeen leaders' quarrels over control cast the nation into a state of civil war. Now the barbaric Taliban were decimating what might be left of human decency and morale in that land. Zweeta's father had done all he could to get out of Afghanistan and find a way to send for his family later.

He went profoundly in debt to secure an escort out of the country—the illegal back door to the West. He was smuggled out and went on the run, from country to country, until he finally found refuge in a country that would accept him. It was part of his plan to get his beloved family out of Afghanistan to a place where they might have hope for a better life and a future.

Zweeta and her family had waited as refugees in Pakistan for the day they would be able to join their father. They weren't alone; there were approximately 2 million Afghans in Pakistan refugee settlements who had fled the hopelessness of their own land. Zweeta was among the lucky few who would actually find this better life in the West. She would probably never return to Pakistan or Afghanistan. When she told me good-bye she asked me to look after her Aunt Zarmeena, who would stay behind with her husband and children.

My first meeting with my new charge was awkward at best. She seemed extremely shy. I wanted to be faithful to the promise I had given. After all, I knew how important it was to have others look after my own family, who lived so far away from me. But as I painfully struggled to make any type of conversation with her, I wondered if I would ever become the friend her niece had asked me to be. There was absolutely no initial connection between us.

To make matters worse, Zarmeena's youngest son was a challenge. I like children, but he was one of the rudest boys I had ever met—a 5-year-old package of disrespect and bad manners. *Lord*, I thought, *Can't You put them with someone else? This isn't going to work.*

Over the next few months I spent a lot of time with Zarmeena and her two youngest children. It was a time of discovery, and the walls began to come down. Amazingly she became a close friend, someone I actually enjoyed spending time with. I could now sincerely thank God that I was asked to look out for her. I also came to the place where I could tease and joke with her son, at times playfully throwing him in the air. I discovered that a little time and love would take care of the rudeness, which was nothing more than a manifestation of his own shyness around me as a foreign woman.

Zarmeena slowly began to confide in me. Her heart was breaking that day I first met her. Everyone was celebrating her niece's family's immigration status, and she was feeling very alone in the world. Her own parents had been killed during the time of the Soviet invasion, and her younger brothers died in the ensuing civil war. Her sister had fled west to Iran to escape the fierce rule of the Taliban. Now her oldest brother who had raised her was heading oceans away. She had none of her own immediate family to care for her and her children.

In societies like Afghanistan the immediate family plays an extremely important role—something hard for us independent Americans to grasp. Here she was, a refugee in another land, bidding a forever farewell to the family who loved her the most. Though she was married and had children, this separation was very difficult for her. I began to understand her sorrow and extreme quietness that day. She just needed a friend.

After the fall of the Taliban, Zarmeena's family moved back to their beloved homeland. They were shocked by what had happened since they had left. Her husband, one of 18 children (his father had two wives), took this extremely hard. With hundreds of thousands returning to Afghanistan, the capital, Kabul, swelled from its usual 1 million plus to some 3 million. Unable to find work and care for his family, he became discouraged and depressed. He left the country, leaving Zarmeena to care for her four children alone.

During this time she began to show interest in my beliefs, Christianity in general and Christ in particular. We watched the *Jesus* film and she asked some questions. I shared with her that knowing God was more than just an intellectual pursuit and doing good works. God loved her personally and cared about the very things that were deep in her heart. As we reclined against the floor cushions on my bedroom floor and sipped tea, I gently asked her about these things.

First, she was concerned about her only sister, who had fled to Iran to escape the Taliban's tyranny. With Afghans going here and there and an infrastructure in shambles, the sisters had lost contact with each other. "God knows where your sister is," I said. "Let's pray." And so we did, in Jesus' name.

A week later she came beaming into my house. After more than seven years her sister had finally made contact with her. Their phone call lasted three minutes before they were cut off. All they did was cry. But they were tears of joy.

Her other main concern was her mind. Like many Afghans, she had seen bloodshed and experienced oppression. She had suffered great loss and much trauma. "The Holy Spirit can come in and heal your pain," I told her. "God wants to help your mind and your memory, and He wants to heal the pain caused by the trauma you have experienced." We prayed, and God slowly began to comfort her, taking away some of her fears and hurt.

Though hesitant at first because of her inability to focus or remember, she began reading the Word.

This day, sitting in my bedroom, she heard the testimony of how an Iranian Muslim lady had accepted Christ years before. The truth she had been learning, this testimony, and the answered prayers came together to make this her day. She prayed to accept Christ. I wasn't sure that it had really happened until I asked her to describe to me what had just occurred. She said she felt so light and free that it was as if the carpet we were sitting on was flying. Isn't that an apt description of how we should feel when the Holy Spirit washes our sins away?

Zarmeena's husband calls her occasionally. My ongoing prayer is that he will come home to his family, and that he too will accept Christ and experience release from the hurts and burdens that caused him to leave. The God who met Zarmeena on a carpet on a foreigner's bedroom floor wants to journey with her husband through his own exhilarating experience of salvation and healing. The Afghan flying carpet ride is for everyone who believes!

Afghan children

Afghan village children

Kabul merchant

Young Afghans

16

A village elder

Chapter Sixteen

COSTLY FAITH

*By Richard Newmann**

"In fact, everyone who wants to live a godly life in Christ Jesus will be persecuted" (2 Timothy 3:12).

Christians in Silk Road countries face dire consequences if they convert from Islam. Probably nowhere else are the consequences more dire than in Iran, the world's only Islamic theocracy. There, if you convert from Islam, you will not only pay with your reputation and your livelihood, but you may be put to death by the government. Many have to flee the country for their lives, bringing nothing with them. Many go from prosperity to life as a refugee, constantly looking over their shoulders for fear they may be deported or killed. These are the stories of two such men.

Davoud

Davoud was a prosperous businessman and a devout

Muslim in Iran. He even read the Koran in Arabic. One night he had a life-changing dream. In it he saw himself preaching from the Injil (the New Testament) in his own language (Farsi). He was unaware that an Injil existed in Farsi. Then a man with a robe, a beard and a staff came alongside him and began walking with him. He thought it might be John the Baptist who is revered as a prophet in Islam. Then, a great storm arose. The bearded man asked God what was happening and God answered, "A new revolution is starting." This man turned and looked at Davoud. At that moment, he knew the man was Jesus. Jesus said, "You are to be a leader in this revolution." Jesus then took a step up a staircase and Davoud followed him. At that moment, he woke up sobbing intensely. His wife told him that he should pray and God would show him what the dream meant.

Davoud and his wife had a neighbor who had become a Christian. They told him about the dream. The believer convinced Davoud to come see his pastor the following night. The pastor told Davoud that God wanted to have a relationship with him and wanted Davoud to become His follower. Davoud just laughed. "I will never leave Islam," he said. Believing Christians to be the ones who are deceived, Davoud confronted the pastor for five hours, firing question after question at him.

Although Davoud spoke the questions in anger and

aggression, the pastor always answered his questions peacefully. At the end of the meeting, a man and a woman prayed for Davoud in Farsi. He was amazed because he had only ever heard prayers in Arabic, and those prayers seemed so personal, as though God would hear them. The pastor gave Davoud a New Testament, also in Farsi—the first he had ever seen except for in his dream. He took it home and placed it by his bed. It stayed there, unread, for several weeks.

Over that time, Davoud fought with God. His wife read the New Testament and begged him to read it. He finally relented, reading with the Bible in one hand and the Koran in the other. What he did not know was that, after reading the New Testament, his wife and children had become believers. But because he was a strict Muslim and an angry, confrontational man, they were afraid to tell him.

He had two more dreams. In one a man laid his hands on him and prayed for him twice, telling him that he was at the crossroads of faith and must make a decision. In the dream his son burst into the room and begged him to say something if he believed, but to say nothing if he didn't. This dream greatly troubled him. He began wandering the streets talking to God out loud. "God, if You want something from me, tell me," he prayed. "If not, then let go of me!" His wife was afraid that he was losing his mind, but the pastor assured her that God was indeed talking to him.

His final dream was of a book given to him by two hands out of the darkness. In the book were Koranic verses in Arabic followed by verses in Farsi from the New Testament. As Davoud passed his hands over the words, the verses in Arabic disappeared leaving only the verses in Farsi. He woke up in a panic. He jumped out of bed and rang the neighbor's doorbell at 2:30 a.m. "I must talk to the pastor tonight," he stammered.

Although his neighbor convinced him to wait until the morning, he was very anxious. "What if I die tonight?" Davoud asked. He spent a sleepless night waiting for the morning to come.

The next morning the pastor met with Davoud and led him to Christ. For the first time in his life he had peace. All of his anger left and everyone in his family saw the change. His wife asked him what happened and he told her he had become a Christian. Both she and his children shouted out loud for joy when he told them this.

Ismoil

Ismoil studied the Koran for five years and served in a mosque. But then he began to drink to ease the emptiness he felt in his life. He knew he was a sinner, because it is against Islam for a Muslim to drink alcohol. He stopped praying and reading the Koran, and after that had no desire to pray or study anymore. He was an angry man, like Davoud, and frequently fought with his wife and family.

Through a series of events, his wife became a believer and convinced him to come to church. He agreed to come just once, but only to prove that his wife was wrong. At the church, he angrily confronted the pastor.

"Please, just hold your peace until after we pray and sing," the pastor responded, "and then if you want to ask any questions you may." Ismoil agreed. As the people prayed and sang, he felt a peace come over him like he had never known.

At the end of this time, he said to the pastor, "I just have one question. Is Jesus the Son of God or not?"

The pastor smiled. "Yes, Jesus is the Son of God," he said.

Ismoil thought for a moment. Then he said, "OK, I want to be a Christian." He, like Davoud, became a changed man. His anger and emptiness left him. He stopped abusing his family and alcohol.

From here, the stories of Davoud and Ismoil are remarkably similar. They became bold in their faith and attended church regularly. They shared their faith with others and studied God's Word. It was not long before the secret police found out that they had become believers. They brought them in for interrogations. They told them if they did not return to Islam they would be arrested and hanged—the penalty for an apostate.

Neither one of them recanted. The interrogations eventually stopped. Then one day the secret police showed up at each of their homes, and told them they needed to talk to them one more time. Their families were told they would return shortly. But it was a month before their families saw them again. They were brought to prison this time and put in solitary confinement in a cell so small that there was barely room to lie down. They were constantly interrogated and tortured, but they never turned from their faith. They told their accusers they would never leave Jesus and that they were ready to die.

At one point Davoud was brought blindfolded into a room and questioned again. When he spoke the name of Jesus, one of his interrogators struck him in the face. He then told the unseen man that Jesus teaches that if someone strikes you on your right cheek, to turn the other to him as well, at which point he was struck on the other side of his face. He then heard the man who had hit him storm out of the room and slam the door.

When he came back into the room, Davoud asked him, "Do you understand why you raised your hand against me?"

He answered, "Of course I know. I did it because I was angry at what you said."

Davoud replied, "No. You raised your hand against me because the name of Jesus is so powerful that even unbelievers must raise their hands at the mention of His name."

Another time a learned mullah (an Islamic teacher) was sent to pressure one of the men to return to Islam. For two and a half hours the mullah tried to change his mind and convince him to revert. But for every question the mullah had, the young believer had an answer, even using the Koran to show that Jesus was Lord. The only response the mullah could muster was, "You are crazy!"

Finally, at the end of a month, each was brought before a judge who told them that their case was now closed; their sentence was death.

But then the judge said something amazing: "Even

though your sentence is death, we are releasing you. You are not to pray, attend church, read your Bible, talk to other believers or talk to anyone about your faith. If you do, you will find the sentence carried out quickly."

They could not understand why they had received this reprieve. Later they learned that so many others had become believers the government was afraid to carry out a death sentence for fear of violence.

But when Davoud and Ismoil returned home, they found that the government still did everything they could to make their lives miserable. They closed their businesses and took away their drivers' licenses. Davoud was kicked out of the home he rented and was told that his children would not be allowed to attend the university. They also received death threats.

They knew that they had to leave the country and everything they loved there. They currently are refugees in another country. But they both have the hope that things will change soon and someday they will return to lead others in Iran to faith in Jesus Christ.

Naan, the bread that is a Central Asian staple

Market scenes

17

The front entrance of
Protestant International Church

Chapter Seventeen

RESTORATION IN ISLAMABAD

By Keith Talkington

I am going to restore worship in this place, because I am a healer and I can heal anything that is broken. There was no mistaking God's voice. He had plans for this church.

As I stood outside a classroom in the basement of the Protestant International Church (PIC) in Islamabad, Pakistan, I knew this for certain. A terrorist grenade attack here had claimed the lives of four worshippers and injured more than 40 others. Despite this, God had plans beyond repairing the damaged building. He would also bring healing to the body of believers who call PIC their church home.

This was not the first word that the Holy Spirit had spoken to me concerning the church. Two weeks after the attack, Mark Hausfeld, area director for Central Eurasia, called me at my apartment in Naperville, Illinois. Mark had just returned from Islamabad after two weeks of counseling and debriefing with the survivors of the attack. Mark said, "I want you and your wife to consider going to Islamabad to pastor the Protestant International Church. The church is without a pastor and the congregation has been scattered after a terrorist threw six hand grenades into the congregation during the morning worship service on March 17, 2002. Three of the grenades exploded, killing the wife and teenage daughter of a U.S. diplomat, an Afghan man and a 17-year-old Pakistani girl."

As Mark was speaking the Holy Spirit assured me with these words: *You and your wife go to Islamabad and volunteer to be the pastors of PIC and I will take care of you.* That June, my wife and I spent two weeks in Islamabad talking with the leaders of the church. Many of the expatriate members had evacuated to their homelands. Those left in Islamabad were in various stages of grief, healing and recovery. During this time, God spoke His message to us about restoring worship at PIC. The church leadership invited us and we agreed to become the pastors of the church.

While we were in the States preparing for the move to Islamabad, the church met on Sundays in various homes, changing the schedule regularly as a precaution against any further terrorism. Meanwhile, repairs on the badly damaged sanctuary were underway.

Donations from churches around the world helped pay for the reconstruction. A Korean church sent funds and equipment to entirely refurnish the sanctuary. One man came from the U.S. to supervise the construction of fences and walls around the property to provide the needed security. He was followed by another from Scotland. A retired pastor came from the U.S. to give two months of spiritual leadership in the fall of 2002.

On March 9, 2003, nearly a year after the attack, the congregation moved back into the remodeled sanctuary. Shortly after the reopening of the church, Blanche and I arrived to assume the pastoral duties. At that time 30 people were attending the morning service. By August attendance had grown to 80 and in September nearly 100 people were in church on Sunday morning, including 25 children in our Sunday School. Young families were moving back to Islamabad and joining our congregation. God was indeed restoring worship at PIC.

God was also at work restoring the worshippers who had been in the attack. In the months following the opening of the church facility many of these returned to Islamabad. Often they would come by the church during the week just to "take a look." The scene was often repeated as I accompanied each one on their "walk through." At the entrance of the sanctuary they would stop and comment how beautifully the church had been restored. Almost reluctant to enter the place that held such terrifying memories they would stand at the back of the sanctuary and gaze out over the empty room. Then they would point to the location where they sat when the grenades exploded. Sometimes they would walk to the place and sit down. It was then that they would cry. Some sat for a few seconds, some for up to an hour. Many would pray and thank God for saving their lives. When it was over they left, often without further comment. Some would return the next Sunday to worship; others did not.

On March 17 of 2004 and 2005 we gathered together just to remember. Many spoke of things that happened that day and how God had been at work since then.

"Before the attack we did not know each other. Now we are a family."

"I hid under a chair and asked Jesus to save me."

"A grenade landed under the chair next to me. It did not explode."

"Our car had a flat tire on the way to church and we could not attend that morning."

In her testimony, Rushani Weerasooriya writes:

"I won't ever forget that death-like smell, or the color of human flesh and blood; I'll always remember what it was like to watch someone die, and I guess those pounding noises will echo in me for a while. But since I am still alive I know my life must have a purpose . . . my one desire now, is to fulfill it, for I can't help but be grateful to have been spared. My soul is now at peace because in me there is a new urge to love this world like Christ loves me."

Easter Sunday, March 27, 2005. Three years have passed since the grenade attack at PIC. One hundred twenty worshippers gather to celebrate the resurrection of Jesus Christ. In the same sanctuary where deafening blasts spread death, terror and confusion, the PIC choir, consisting of believers from Nigeria, the United States, the Philippines and Pakistan, boldly proclaims in song, "It's still the cross that frees from sin and sets the captive free. . . ."

Evidence that God is restoring and renewing this congregation comes midway through the service. Three babies are brought forward for blessing. In November the mother of the babies had come to Islamabad from Kabul to give birth to quintuplets. Two of the babies died shortly after birth and the mother died a few days later. Ladies from the congregation cared for the remaining three for the next four months, praying each baby would sense the presence of the Holy Spirit. The father would be coming from Kabul the next week to take his two sons and daughter home. The congregation prays that each baby will come to know the message of salvation.

At the close of the day, the words stir in my heart once more, *I am going to restore worship in this place.* God has been true to His word.

Members survey the damage after the attack

A security guard now patrols the church property

Shairat

Chapter Eighteen

SHAIRAT'S SERENDIPITIES
As told to Lynda Hausfeld

Shairat was born a Kurd, one of a people group who originate from the geographical region where Turkey, Iran and Iraq share borders. Some scholars say that the Kurds are the descendents of the Medes of the Medo-Persian Empire, in the prophet Daniel's day. Today they are a people without a home in their own land; they are the world's largest people group who don't have their own nation.

Shairat was raised in Almaty, Kazakhstan. When Shairat was 8 years old, her mother fled her abusive marriage and abandoned her and four other siblings to the care of their difficult father. Unable to take care of them himself, he put the three girls into a government orphanage. Shairat waited three years for her father or mother to come back for her, but nobody came. In the orphanage she suffered serious abuse at the hands of a very rough caregiver. Then, after three years, she and her siblings were reunited with the remarried father and a new stepmother. Still, the abuse continued. A number of times she was beaten until she lost consciousness. The trauma resulted in permanent damage to her eyes.

All her young life Shairat resented her mother's disappearance. She learned to despise her for the years of torment she endured as a result of her abandonment.

Shairat's difficulties stretched into her late adolescent years. At age 18 she was abducted and forced to marry a man who had been an acquaintance. Wife stealing is a common practice in some Central Eurasian countries. If a man is unable to pay a dowry, or if he is rejected by the girl he desires or by her parents, he will often kidnap her. In Shairat's culture, a Muslim girl who has spent a night outside the protection of her family would be considered damaged goods and a shame to the family. She would be unable to return to the father's house. Essentially, the girl's family forfeits the daughter to her new husband.

One day, Shairat was waiting for a bus with her friend at a city stop. The girl's 27-year-old male cousin pulled up in a car and offered them a lift. They both got into the car, but before the car started, her friend jumped out. The cousin drove off with Shairat. It wasn't long before she realized she was being abducted for marriage purposes, and that her friend had betrayed her to this cousin. She pled for her release, to no avail.

Now her husband against her will, the man locked Shairat up in a room for three months. She was there for his pleasure, and all she knew was the pain of his violations against her. After three months this man accepted employment out of town, and would only come home once a week. He felt he must allow Shairat to have a key, in return for her promise that she would not run away.

Shairat knew that if she were able to escape, she could not go back to her own family. In her culture, if she showed up at home, the father might feel pressed to kill her to restore the family honor. Even so, her despair drove her to escape this husband and family, and to flee into an unknown future. The streets seemed more hospitable than this man and the place he had kept her.

Shairat was pregnant at the time.

She went back to the city, and literally knocked on doors to see if someone would take her in. Eventually a woman who was an alcoholic took her in for about a month. One day she ran into a cousin at a bus stop, who promised her that if she returned to her father's house, he would not kill her. Pregnant and desperate, she returned to her father, where amidst continued abuse, she gave birth to little Suliman.

For the next two years Shairat took whatever work she could find. She crossed paths with some Baptist believers, who led her to the Lord. Through very difficult circumstances her faith grew, and it finally became known to her family that she had become a Christ-follower.

This time her father brought out the special knife used for the *Qurban* (a yearly practiced Muslim animal sacrifice) and tried to kill her with it. Her brother overpowered her father and she escaped.

Shairat wound up at the Teen Challenge Center in Kazakhstan, and asked for a job there. When they found out that she spoke Russian, Kazakh, Kurdish and some Turkish, they took her in. After a season of work at the Teen Challenge Center, Shairat's Australian Assemblies of God mentors recognized her potential and her heart for ministry. They encouraged her to complete Bible and ministry training at Silk Road Theological Institute, just a three-hour drive from Almaty. She did so, and graduated with a diploma in Christian Ministry.

Trouble had followed her into her early adult years, but now Christ was ordaining her every step.

Only a few weeks prior to her graduation, a young man who had graduated from the theological institute a few years earlier approached her for some information. He had heard that she was a Kurd, and he had recently felt God's call to minister to a Kurdish settlement that was less than 20 miles out of Bishkek. It was an unreached settlement, among which there were no known believers. This young man asked Shairat for some cultural tips— anything she might be able to tell him that would help him to gain favor and an audience among them. He knew nothing about Kurds except that God was calling him to them.

Shairat, now gregarious and quite fearless, suggested that she would be willing to accompany him to the village to meet these people. What she was about to face in this village, however, would test her faith to its core.

Shairat and Denis visited the settlement together, where she met with the ladies, and he met with the men. Shairat surprised her Kurdish hosts with news of her faith in Christ, because this particular group of Kurds prided themselves in the fact that there were only Muslims among them. They became very interested in her family background, and she unreservedly answered their many questions.

As Shairat was telling her story, a young lady who had also lived in Almaty put some facts together and suddenly said to her, "Shairat, you are my niece!" Shairat had never seen her before. Moments later, a half-brother ran to her and threw his arms around her as he wept and shouted,

"You are my sister!" She was absolutely shocked.

For 22 years Shairat had not known where her mother had gone. Now, just a few miles outside of Bishkek, where the Lord had directed her to prepare for ministry, she was learning that at least 30 of her relatives and her mother all lived in the same vicinity!

In disbelief Shairat made her way back to Silk Road Theological Institute and approached David Broberg, the director.

"I have to talk to you," she said, and her throat poured out her heart's story. "David, I don't know my mother. I was taught to hate her. I don't even love her."

David listened and could see God's hand in this marvelous unraveling of events. He encouraged her to meet her mother. It was no accident that she was living in Kyrgyzstan and the young pastor who needed her help had unknowingly taken her to her relatives. It was all in God's timing. He was using magnificently ordained serendipities to redeem a broken past and offer hope to many futures.

A week later Shairat found David in a hallway and grabbed his arm. "I saw my mother yesterday, and I love her."

When Shairat and her mother embraced for the first

time after 22 years, God miraculously healed Shairat's hurt. Shairat's mother pled for forgiveness, and Shairat gave it. Shairat learned that her mother's family were drug dealers and thieves; but she knew the Lord was giving her opportunity to share His love with them.

The Lord spoke strongly to Shairat through one of her last classes at Silk Road Theological Institute. It was a class on soteriology, the study of salvation. She became keenly aware that her whole family needed Jesus, and her burden for them intensified. Since their only means of salvation would be Jesus, she decided to take Him to them. She swallowed childhood fears and moved home to her father's house to witness to them, and to pray for them. Before long, her father, who had only cursed her before, blessed her. She knew God was reaching him.

Shairat has recently heeded the call to full-time ministry among the Kurds in Kyrgyzstan. Now, two years after she found and had the privilege of reaching members of both sides of her family for Christ, Shairat shines Jesus into her Kurdish community as well. Because she had been kidnapped and unlawfully held against her will, the first marriage was not legally binding. She has found a godly life partner, and at the reading of this story, will have married and begun a new family of her own. It seems that, now, Shairat's life is one serendipity after another. All of them God-ordained.

Kazakh horseman

Kazakh mosque

A yurt church

Kurds

Winter in Kazakhstan

AFTERWORD

Now that you have journeyed with us along the ancient routes of the old Silk Road in Central Eurasia, you have had a taste of what life and ministry are like in this historic part of the world. The challenges of ministry in the Silk Road countries may be greater than anywhere else on earth—and today that seems to be truer than ever.

As we were finishing this book, crises were arising in many of our ministry areas. A suicide bomber detonated a bomb close to Protestant International Church in Islamabad. Kabul, Afghanistan, and Peshawar, Pakistan, were volatile, with thousands in the streets protesting. And Teen Challenge had been threatened with violence in both Pakistan and Kyrgyzstan.

But those whom God has called to minister in these difficult places have grown accustomed to such challenges, and they usually take them in stride. On a few occasions they have evacuated or relocated because of imminent danger. But most often these ministers and their families have stayed the course in trying times, and relied on the prayers of God's people. These prayers are desperately needed, both for protection and for the growth of the church. The need for an army of intercessors to support those who are on the front lines of spiritual battle cannot be overemphasized.

It is the hope of the authors of this book that, now that you have become a little familiar with ministry in this part of the world, you will join this army of intercessors. Please consider making the Silk Road countries a regular part of your prayer life. Hold up these men, women, and children, who have given up things that are familiar, comfortable, and convenient in order to engage people in a sometimes-hostile culture with the life-transforming truths of the gospel of Jesus Christ.

You can help to write the sequel to this book, by praying for those you have read about. Your prayers could make the difference in the life of a Nargiza, a Shairat, or a Farhadov Jhun. They could mean salvation to a Mir Muhammad or protection to a Bishop Sergie. They could mean release from prison for a Hamid Pourmand. Your prayers can strengthen those on the front lines to reach people who seem unreachable. And your prayers can help lay the foundation of new churches in these difficult places.

And perhaps you are one of those readers to whom God is speaking about going to the mission field. Allow the Holy Spirit to give you direction. Perhaps He will direct you to the Silk Road . . . to Central Eurasia. If He does, a wonderful adventure awaits you.

If you would like more information about ministry in this part of the world, please email:

mark.hausfeld@hqmail.agmd.org.

Regular updates are also available.

Mark and Lynda Hausfeld at an Attock Teen Challenge Center graduation ceremony

ABOUT THE AUTHORS

*Names marked with an asterisk are pen names used because of security concerns due to the extreme sensitivities in many of these countries.

Mark and Lynda Hausfeld

Mark, Lynda, and their three children have served in Central Eurasia since 1995. They are Assemblies of God World Missions Area Directors for the area. Prior to their service overseas, they pioneered and pastored a church in Chicago. Lynda has a B.A. in English and Spanish, with certification to teach. Mark holds a D.Min. in Urban Missions.

Peyton Alan*

Peyton Alan has served in Central Eurasia with his wife, Clover, and their three children, since 1996. They have planted one church with two congregations. Before missionary service, the Alans served in a variety of ministries in Virginia, from pastoring to youth and children's ministry. Peyton has degrees from Virginia Commonwealth University and Regent University.

Taylor Allen*

Taylor Allen and his wife have been serving in Tajikistan since 1996. They have three children who also call Tajikistan their home. Before moving to Tajikistan, they lived in California and Colorado, serving as church staff and teachers in a Christian school. Taylor holds an M.A. in Education and Cross-Cultural Studies.

David Broberg

David Broberg, a 1967 North Central University graduate, pastored five separate congregations in the United States before his service with Assemblies of God World Missions. He has directed the Silk Road Theological Institute since its beginning in 1996. He and his wife of 40 years have four children and 13 grandchildren.

Troy Caye*

Troy, his wife, and their four children have served in Turkey since 1990.

Lydia Cyrus*

Lydia Cyrus currently lives in Central Eurasia, where she has been serving since 1990. She was born in Iran and grew up in the Philippines, Nepal, Pakistan and Malaysia before returning to the United States to attend a university. She is the founder and CEO of an organization focused on the social, spiritual, and economic uplift of women through education and hospitality. Her passion is to show Muslim women the love of Jesus Christ.

Robert Lee*

Robert Lee spent many years living in various places along the Silk Road. He currently is teaching at an American university and continues to minister in the Middle East and Central Eurasia every year.

Mike and Cindy

Mike and Cindy were Jesus people. They were engaged in 1976. That same year Mike went to India from Europe in an old bus with a group of young people. Cindy ministered in Italy for four years. She then went to India. They were married in Sri Lanka in an Assemblies of God church Mike helped to build. Their oldest son, Reuel, was born in Sri Lanka, their son David, in India and their daughter, Anjali, in Pakistan. Besides taking part in evangelistic work, they worked in leper colonies and slums. Together with an Indian doctor, they started an orphanage and medical work in a needy village area in southern India. Later they went to live and work in Peshawar, Pakistan, where they gave milk to 15,000 Afghan children every day. Now they work in Central Eurasia.

David Murphy *

David Murphy grew up as a son of a missionary in Tunisia, Jordan, Israel and Spain. After graduating from high school in 1992, David went on to receive a B.A. at Central Bible College in Springfield, Missouri. While at CBC he met his wife and they were married in 1996. David and his wife served three years as youth pastors in Kansas and Kentucky. Following this they served for three years as pastors of First Assembly of God in Industry, Illinois. Feeling a call from God to serve in the former Soviet Union they received their missionary appointment in 2002. They have three children and now live in Baku, Azerbaijan. In Azerbaijan, David is working with the newly formed church and is currently involved in printing a Christian newspaper. David works with Pastor Jhun in Azerbaijan in the areas of youth and worship.

Richard Newmann *

Richard Newmann and his wife have served full time in a Muslim context for two years. They have three children.

They have served together in the ministry for 14 years as pastors, staff pastors, and in other leadership positions. Richard also has secular experience as an entrepreneur, IT specialist, and as a manager for a Fortune 500 company. Fifteen years ago God planted a vision in the hearts of Richard and his wife to reach the lost in Iran. They hope to move to Iran when God opens the doors.

Kathryn Dawn O'Malley *

Kathryn Dawn O'Malley has been working in Western Pakistan and Afghanistan since 1998. She is single and is an appointed special long-term AGWM worker.

Keith Talkington

Keith and his wife, Blanche, from the United States, served in Japan for 22 years before becoming the pastors of the Protestant International Church in 2003. They have two sons and one daughter. The Talkingtons currently reside in Islamabad, Pakistan.

Timothy Virnon*

Timothy Virnon was trained as a geologist and worked for a number of years in the oil industry. He and his wife served for the past 10 years with a christian relief and development organization in Central Eurasia.

Ken Horn

Ken Horn, D.Min., is a minister, author, and managing editor of *Today's Pentecostal Evangel*.

PHOTO CREDITS

Dana Dominguez:
Pages 32, 33, 39, 40, 41b, 54, 60a, 70a, 72, 130, 135-137, 144, 145, 156, 163a, 204-206a, 207

Ken Horn:
Pages 14, 31, 41a, 42, 51-53, 60b, 61a, 96, 97a, 99a, 109, 146, 153-155, 174-176, 185-188, 195, 212

Eric Nelis:
Pages 128, 129

Other photos submitted by contributing writers and other Central Eurasia missionaries and colleagues.

ORDER INFORMATION

For a complete list of books
offered by Onward Books, Inc.
and an order form, please call or write:

Onward Books, Inc.
4848 South Landon Court
Springfield, MO 65810
417-890-7465

ISBN: 1-880689-13-8

Or visit our Web site at:
www.onwardbooks.com